HERBLOCK
AT LARGE

HERBLOCK
AT LARGE

"LET'S GO BACK A LITTLE..."
AND OTHER CARTOONS
WITH COMMENTARY BY
HERBERT BLOCK

PANTHEON BOOKS NEW YORK

All rights reserved under International and Pan-American
Copyright Conventions. Published in the United States by
Pantheon Books, a division of Random House, Inc., New
York, and simultaneously in Canada by Random House of
Canada Limited, Toronto.

The cartoons first appeared in *The Washington Post*.

Library of Congress Cataloging-in-Publication Data

Block, Herbert, 1909–
    Herblock at large: ''Let's go back a little'' and other
cartoons with commentary by Herbert Block
    1. United States—Politics and government—
1981—Caricatures and cartoons. 2. Reagan,
Ronald—Caricatures and cartoons. 3. American wit
and humor, Pictorial. I. Title.
E876.B58   1987   973.927'0207   87-42914
ISBN 0-394-56569-X

Manufactured in the United States of America

First Edition

TO JEAN AND ED RICKARD

Contents

Again—

"Thanks" is a good enough word for acknowledging directions down the street or the passing along of salt and pepper shakers, but it seems too little for the kind of help I've had on this book—especially from my associate Jean Rickard. She worked from beginning to end, day and night, editing, preparing and organizing manuscript and cartoons and *everything* connected with the book. No one else could have done so much or made it possible to meet the deadline.

Special assistant Donna Canzano did an ace job of researching and also put in long hours on all the organizing work, with help from Patty Moriarty.

David Hoffman and Robin Meszoly, two of the best and most knowledgeable journalists anywhere, are also among the most generous. On book manuscripts as well as on daily cartoons, they have taken time out to edit drafts and give invaluable advice. Speaking of generosity, Haynes Johnson is another who finds time in his own hectic schedule to look over my roughs for cartoons and text.

Bob and Jane Asher and Doree Lovell have been over this course before and once more the words have benefited from their special skills with blue pencils.

Dan Morgan and George C. Wilson lent their expertise on particular chapters.

Until I think of something better, thanks again—thanks ever so much.

H.B.

What's Going On Here?

In William Saroyan's play *The Time of Your Life,* there is a character who mutters, at intervals, "No foundation. All the way down the line." We have been in a period of no foundations, which, if they don't go all the way down the line, go pretty far. It has been the Era of Cotton Candy and of Beautiful Sandcastles, of Hollywood on the Potomac—and of the Great Gaps that separate appearance from reality. Like the characters in animated cartoons who walk off cliffs and continue walking without any visible means of support, our national leaders have defied the law of gravity—temporarily, at least.

In six years, the world's greatest nation has gone from creditor to World's Greatest Debtor, with the world's greatest trade imbalance.

In the federal government, there has never been so much talk about morality accompanied by so much corruption, so much talk of standing tall while creeping small, so much lawbreaking by law-and-order politicians, so much talk of fiscal responsibility while running up record deficits. Never before has there been so great a chasm between words and deeds, so much raising of flags while lowering national standards.

High finance has reached an altitude where it has separated completely from services and productivity. Individual enterprises have been swallowed up in mergers that have been swallowed up in megamergers that have given way to takeovers and greenmail operations. In these, billions of dollars change hands quickly without any business having been conducted other than making plans to grab billions of dollars.

Executives heap huge incomes on themselves—often at the cost of employees with modest salaries. High rollers are concerned only with a bottom line, which is often right there at the bottom of the barrel. A

millionaire was once a person whose total worth was a million dollars
—enough to live a lifetime of luxury. No longer. A millionaire today is
a person who makes a million a year—just enough to qualify for the
new millionaire's club alongside some Wall Streeters and real estate
developers who do even better. Some business executives also run up
higher scores with salaries, stock options and bonuses. And in case of
sudden difficulties, these high fliers have golden parachutes.

Also dealing in megabucks have been the TV evangelists who decry
sin and who are up there in direct communication with God—while at
a more mundane level, they rake in millions a year to keep themselves
on TV—and sometimes to keep themselves living in the high style to
which they have made themselves accustomed.

The gap between high and low exists physically on crowded airlines,
where takeoffs and arrivals don't match the times billed in the sched-
ules, and the blue yonder is not as wild as some of the airports where
travelers find themselves grounded.

While high finance has gone its separate way from business in the
private sector, huge spending outlays have also outrun results in some
of the government's big-ticket items. Record arms spending has failed
to produce the best national defense, and record agriculture subsidies
have not saved family farms from the auction block.

These have not been "the best of times and the worst of times."
They have been the most incredible of times—and featuring high officials who have been highly incredible.

What we seem to have is a schizoid society—perhaps best illus-
trated by polls during the Iran-contra scandal that showed a sizable
majority of Americans felt President Reagan was lying—while a sizable majority in the same polls also felt he was honest.

Incredible situations often bring up speculation about what a man
from Mars would think. Anyone who has been around awhile can now
be a man from Mars. *What's going on here?*

LAND OF PLENTY

"I THINK YOU GENTLEMEN ARE ALL ACQUAINTED"

GENERAL DYNAMICS

GENERAL ELECTRIC

GENERAL WASTE

GENERAL INCOMPETENCE

©1985 HERBLOCK

4/4/85

"DIRECT FROM THE GUN LOBBY — IT'S SATURDAY NIGHT DEAD"

CHEAPO SPECIALS

©1985 HERBLOCK

10/10/85

"REMEMBER—OUT OF EVERY DOLLAR SPENT FOR DEFENSE, SOME PART OF IT GOES FOR ACTUAL DEFENSE"

MAKE-WORK PROGRAMS FOR ARMS COMPANIES

MALFUNCTIONING ARMS PROGRAMS

BARGAINING CHIPS

$7,000 COFFEE POTS AND OTHER WASTE

Pentagon Procurement

©1985 HERBLOCK

1/30/85

SAFETY NET

©1985 HERBLOCK

4/18/85

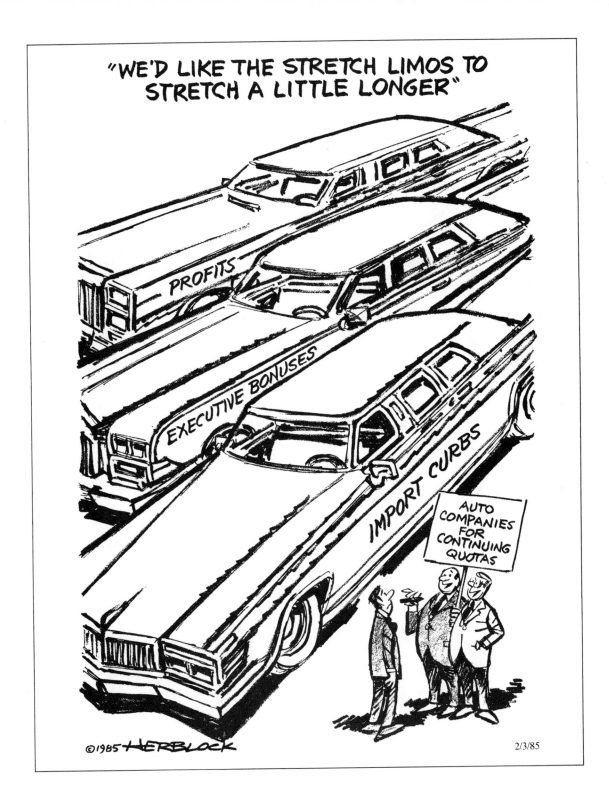

"IT'S A FAMOUS OLD CURE CALLED BLEEDING"

"AND REMEMBER, THERE IS NO SUCH THING AS FREE LUNCH — UNLESS YOU CAN CLAIM TO HAVE DISCUSSED BUSINESS"

©1985 HERBLOCK
7/21/85

U.S. Becomes World's No. 1 Debtor Nation

6//29/86

"AND ALL THAT FUSS ABOUT TV EVANGELISTS"

©1987 HERBLOCK
3/31/87

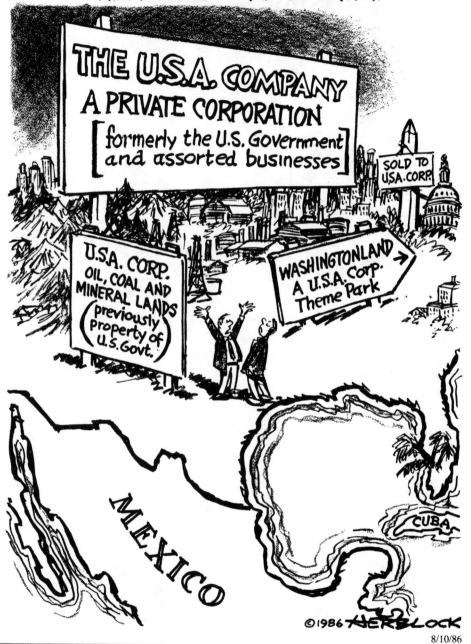

"HARVEY DOESN'T LIKE IT"

WASHINGTON D.C., 1986

SITE OF PROPOSED
NEW ADDITION TO
THE PENTAGON
Est. cost:
$450,000,000.00

"THE U.S. AIR TRAVEL SAFETY RECORD HAS BEEN VERY GOOD. THE U.S. AIR TRAVEL SAFETY RECORD HAS BEEN VERY GOOD... THIS IS A RECORDING..."

8/13/87

LIBRARY OF CONGRESS
NEW EARLIER
CLOSING HOURS
DUE TO BUDGET CUTS:

3/23/86

"AS IT SAYS HERE IN THE SCRIPTURES SOMEWHERE—THEY SHALL BEAT THEIR PLOWSHARES INTO SWORDS"

2/6/85

Math

Class, we'll start with something simple. If you have six apples and you meet a little boy who has two apples . . . Yes, Ronald? Yes, they could be bombs, but we prefer to use apples . . . And the little boy has two apples . . . No, Ronald, you don't take away the little boy's two apples . . . Well, you shouldn't assume that he'll try to take yours. What we're trying to do here is to add . . . No, you don't make the little boy go and get some more apples. The little boy is *not* necessarily lazy, Ronald; he has only two apples. So both of you together have how many apples? No, the answer is not 22, Ronald. I know, but *saying* you have that many doesn't make it so. Well, somebody would probably find out, that's why. Now, let's give someone else a chance . . . William Gray here . . . Eight apples, that's correct. I didn't say William ate the apples, Ronald, and stop throwing spitballs at him. I think we'd better try something else.

Let's suppose that we have a store, and let's say that Oko Noko here has a brother who owns a store across the street. Oko's brother makes very nice things, and we buy $100 worth of his things. But we don't have too much that Mr. Noko wants so he only buys $20 worth of what we have . . . Richard . . . Richard Gephardt, stop pushing Oko . . . We are trying to do some figures here . . . That's right, William, the difference is eighty dollars . . . No, Richard, we do not tell Mr. Noko to give us back eighty dollars . . . No, Ronald, we do not get your Uncle Sammy's credit card and write his name on it . . . Boys, stop pushing Oko; we are trying to do some figures here. Everybody sit down. We'll try something without apples or people.

We'll take another example of money. Suppose it costs a dollar to collect every hundred dollars of taxes . . . Yes, I said taxes and don't make that noise with your mouth, Ronald, it's not nice . . . Now suppose we decide that we will cut down the number of people collecting taxes . . . and we save $100—but we lose $10,000 in collections. Are we saving money or losing money? Anyone? William Bradley? Losing money, that's right . . . Ronald, stop shooting peas at William.

Now we'll see what you can do with big numbers. I'll write a very big number on the blackboard. We'll call it National Debt, end of 1980: with a dollar sign in front: $930,000,000,000. And now here is an even bigger number. Let's see if we can get it all on the blackboard. There —we'll call this National Debt, July 1987, and this one is $2,280,000,000,000. Now, can someone tell me the difference between these two numbers . . . Anyone? No, Ronald, it's not a crazy number and please let's give someone else a chance to respond. David Stockman? That's right . . . the second number is over 2 trillion—more than twice the size of the first one. Very good, David . . . Ronald, stop kicking David. And what in the world did you two do with your math books that makes them look so funny? You cooked them? Well, you shouldn't have done that. This is a math class, not a cooking class. *NOW,* let's imagine that debt—or total deficit—is a greeeaaat big hole in the ground. What do we do about that hole? Yes, Ronald . . . No, we do not buy lots of bombs and blow up the hole. That only makes the hole bigger. All right, Ronald, you have another answer. You write on a piece of paper No More Deficit. That's nice, but it doesn't *do* anything, does it? No, it doesn't make any difference if it's written on a legal pad. I think we'd better call on someone else. James Wright? You'd try to begin filling up the hole. Ronald, stop throwing things at James and the boys on the other side of the aisle.

Class, how much more time do we have today? Where is the clock that's supposed to be on the wall? Does anyone . . . Ronald, what do you mean you sold the clock? How could you have sold the school clock? You thought the clock would be better with private hands . . . This is serious, Ronald—that was public property. Really! Does anyone here know what time it is?

Anyone? Anyone?

"IF YOU FELLOWS WOULD JUST STUDY THIS PIE CHART—"

1/20/87

PAMPLONA, N.Y.

7/9/86

3/3/85

"HOW DOES HE DO THAT?"

1/9/87

2/15/85

1/16/87

If you can't stand the heat, let somebody else take it.

CONGRESS

BUDGET

©1985 HERBLOCK

4/2/85

MADE IN U.S.A.

BUDGET DEFICIT

TRADE DEFICIT

©1987 HERBLOCK

5/10/87

"DAMN FOREIGNERS!"

IMPORTS

IMPORTS

TRADE DEFICIT

Made in U.S.A.

OVERVALUED DOLLAR

Made in U.S.A.

RECORD FEDERAL DEFICIT

Made in USA

U.S. 85 PROTECTION!

©1985 HERBLOCK

8/4/85

"FOLLOW ME!"

NEW CUTS IN DOMESTIC PROGRAMS

©1985 HERBLOCK

5/2/85

RESCUE PARTY

"BALANCED BUDGET AMENDMENT"

REAGAN DEFICITS

©1985 HERBLOCK

1/22/85

3 KIDS IN COLLEGE

©1985 HERBLOCK

8/25/85

"GOSH—— FOR A MOMENT, I THOUGHT YOU SAID 'LAUNCHES'"

MORE CUTS IN SCHOOL LUNCHES

©1985 HERBLOCK

3/17/85

YOU MAY ALREADY HAVE WON A $1 TRILLION 500 BILLION NATIONAL DEBT

PERSONAL For OCCUPANT U.S.A.

©1984 HERBLOCK

12/30/84

GREAT DISCOVERIES

The New World – 1492

The Pacific — 1513

The Deficit — Post-Election, 1984

11/15/84

"THAT'S VERY GOOD — HOW LONG DID YOU BOIL IT?"

BALANCED BUDGET PROMISES

VOODOO SCHOOL OF ECONOMICS

©1984 HERBLOCK

8/19/84

VOODOO ECONOMICS, ADVANCED COURSE

ADMINISTRATION FISCAL MESS, AS PREDICTED BY DAVID STOCKMAN

BUDGET DEBT

©1986 HERBLOCK

5/4/86

"NOBODY CLAPPED"

SENATE BUDGET COMMITTEE — G.O.P. MAJORITY

REAGAN "IF-YOU-BELIEVE-IN"-FAIRIES BUDGET

©1985 HERBLOCK

3/14/85

1/23/85

"IT SURE BEATS WHAT I USED TO BE"

5/8/86

"LET'S SEE — GIVETH, TAKETH AWAY, GIVETH, GIVETH, TAKETH AWAY —"

8/19/86

TRIVIAL PURSUIT

2/1/85

"WAIT A MINUTE, HONEY — IT MIGHT TAKE ME A WHILE TO GET THE HANG OF THIS"

Talking Tall

"**O**ne of these days!'' Jackie Gleason's Ralph Kramden used to threaten as he waved his fist at Alice. And ''let me at him—I'll moider the bum'' has been shouted by other comedians who were not about to moider anyone. On the screen this has been high comedy. In government, the talk remains tall, but the actions aren't so funny.

From the moment he took office, President Reagan let it be known that there had better not be any fooling around with Uncle Sam. For terrorists our policy would be one of ''swift and effective retribution.'' And they could run but they couldn't hide. But even when we knew where they were hiding, there was no effective retribution. Reagan's administration kept standing smaller, but still talking big—even while covertly crawling in the hope of getting hostages released.

Whether it was facing a budget crunch or meting out justice to terrorists, there were always big words. And at the funerals of American servicemen blown to bits while carrying out foolhardy policies, there were fine and noble words—but still words—and still funerals—which were no substitute for wise policies and deeds.

Whatever the realities, the words marched on to a drum of their own —even when they were at war with themselves.

In the Persian Gulf, during the summer of 1987, we were reflagging Kuwaiti ships to maintain freedom of navigation—although Kuwait was aiding its ally Iraq, the country that had destroyed the most ships in the gulf. We were neutral, but on the side of Iraq—which had hit an American warship. We were preserving the freedom of the seas while trying to keep Russia from playing a larger part in international waters. And President Reagan (who had shown no interest in maintaining energy-saving policies at home) said we were in the gulf to prevent future lines at gas stations—although the original gas lines were caused by Arab embargoes and not by Iran. Little of our oil comes from the Persian Gulf anyhow.

Also—in November 1986, President Reagan told advisers that we needed to aid Iran in its war with Iraq because Iran was "weaker"— when, in fact, it was winning. Then he switched and reflagged Kuwaiti tankers to help Iraq—but this helped Iran by keeping the gulf open so its oil could flow. Everything clear?

What we were doing there was demonstrating a "presence"—which is what we were doing in Lebanon four years earlier when the deaths of more than 260 Americans caused us to lower the flag and withdraw.

We were talking tall, tall, tall.

"One of these days . . . !"

"ANYONE THAT'S EVER HAD THEIR KITCHEN DONE OVER KNOWS THAT IT NEVER GETS DONE AS SOON AS YOU WISH IT WOULD"— Reagan, on the latest failure to provide security.

9/25/84

6/18/85

6/23/85

"WE NEVER GOT TO 'EDUCATE' THAT ONE"

7/2/85

HOME

6/21/85

MESSAGE FROM MALTA

11/26/85

"SAY—WE COULD HIJACK AN AMERICAN PLANE AND TELL THE U.S. TO PUT PRESSURE ON ENGLAND"

6/26/85

"REMEMBER, YOU GET ALONG WITH ME, AND MY BOYS DON'T BOTHER YOUR STORE"

10/16/85

"WHAT DO YOU THINK THIS IS—AN INTELLIGENCE AGENCY?"

6/20/85

"IF ONLY WE HAD MENTAL DETECTORS"

6/27/85

"GEE, I DON'T KNOW ABOUT GOING ABROAD THESE DAYS"

4/20/86

AIR PIRACY

©1985 HERBLOCK
6/28/85

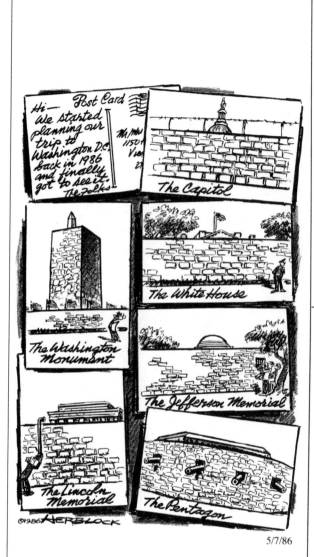

5/7/86

REFLAGGING POLICY

©1987 HERBLOCK

7/1/87

"THEY COME ALONG TO SEE IF THEY CAN FIND A POLICY"

PERSIAN GULF MYSTERY CRUISE

©1987 HERBLOCK

6/25/87

"WE'LL THINK ABOUT THAT TOMORROW"

©1987 HERBLOCK

6/7/87

"OUR REFLAGGING WENT PERFECTLY, BUT SOME SNEAK PUT OUT AN UNFLAGGED MINE"

©1987 HERBLOCK
7/28/87

"I REMEMBER THE REFLAGGING IN LEBANON"

©1987 HERBLOCK
7/5/87

"OOPS"

©1987 HERBLOCK
8/2/87

Angelic Guardians

The country is full of guardians who want to look after us. They are happy and eager to be their brothers' keepers, and want only the keys and cells that go with the keeper's job. An administration, sworn to protect and defend the Constitution, has been out to protect us from sin and our own thoughts about God. It has wanted organized prayer in the public schools, whether the kids and their families want it or not. Its Christian enthusiasm has not extended much to such earthly matters as programs to aid children, who are the most numerous victims of poverty; but this may be due to some misinterpretation of the injunction to "suffer the little children."

Attorney General Edwin Meese, whose interest in godliness may be exceeded only by his chumminess with the founding fathers, maintained that the founders would have thought the Supreme Court's view on separation of church and state to be "somewhat bizarre."

In his efforts to save us from sin, the attorney general approved a report from an official commission on pornography. In the course of its work, this commission had sent, on official stationery, an intimidating letter to 7-Elevens and other chain stores targeting magazines that the stores then removed from their shelves. Later, the FBI raided some video shops in Virginia and Maryland because they were carrying X-rated videos for home viewing. The raid was conducted as part of "a general investigation" without anyone being arrested or charged. The administration may not be so good at protecting us from enemies domestic and foreign, but it is by God determined to protect us from ourselves.

Mr. Meese has been noble and selfless in concentrating our attention on pornography and spiritual concerns, saving us from worrying too much about official investigations of his involvement in major administration scandals.

Some government officials who have been highly vocal in their religiosity have taken a dim view of family planning. If God meant for us to plan families he would have given us more brains than he gave dogs and cats.

Sen. Jesse Helms is among those opposed to family planning; but he has been a strong supporter of Augusto Pinochet, dictator of Chile, who has planned the elimination of a lot of families. Sen. Helms also vigorously supports the tobacco industry, which helps, in a less direct manner, to send people to their Maker earlier than otherwise.

The government has not been alone in saving us from "secular humanism." In some areas, religious fundamentalists have attacked books and schools for not instilling their beliefs into the schoolchildren. In Tennessee, a federal judge not only protected children from passages in *The Diary of Anne Frank* and *The Wizard of Oz*, but ruled that the school should compensate the parents of the children exposed to such matter.

But the administration's strongest ties have been with such high-profile big-audience fundamentalists as television evangelist Jerry Falwell, a political as well as spiritual ally. Falwell, who sounds as if he is buddy-buddy with the Lord, took trips to South Africa and to the Philippines to show his (and presumably the Lord's) buddiness with President P.W. Botha and then-dictator Ferdinand Marcos. In carrying out his and God's wishes on the Philippines, there must have been a faulty connection.

Pat Robertson, another political televangelist, and, as they say, a "brother in Christ," suggested that Christians feel more strongly than others about things like "love of country." Too bad for Americans of other religions and for "freethinkers" such as some of the nation's founders.

In 1987, the televangelists not only sent their messages over the airwaves, but they themselves became part of the news programs. Oral Roberts held the nation in a state of giggling suspense after he declared that God had told him he would be "called home" unless he raised $8 million by a certain date. Thanks to a supportive former dogtrack owner, Roberts made his deadline. And after proving how he could raise funds, Roberts went on to claim that in his work he had also raised the dead—literally. As he told it, he also had God's word that he will play a lead part in the Second Coming. Perhaps he will arrange for network broadcasts. If Roberts is in charge of the Second Coming,

The Event probably would not take place at the Jim and Tammy Bakker Christian Theme Park, which contains a water slide.

But Roberts as a news subject was soon topped by the Bakkers of the PTL (for Praise The Lord—and People That Love) broadcast ministry. Jim was accused by other televangelists of sexual misconduct, and he temporarily turned PTL over to Jerry Falwell, who later read the Bakkers out of the organization. Falwell pleaded for money, and finally took as his text U.S.A. Chapter 11, which finds no sin in holy bankruptcy.

The big TV evangelists raised holy hell with each other, some opposing the Bakkers and others supporting them. On Bakker's side was former Secretary of the Interior and former PTL board member James Watt. Ironically, another supporter of Bakker against Falwell was televangelist Jimmy Swaggart, who earlier had been accused by Bakker of planning a takeover of PTL himself.

The Bakkers, it turned out, had lived very well, even by TV standards. They also received huge salaries and other payments and had at least three homes, among them a large house in Palm Springs and a seldom-used apartment fitted with gold fixtures—in addition to their luxurious house at the ministry.

The public fighting between the televangelists included mentions of "takeovers"—hostile or friendly—appropriate terms for these large-scale financial enterprises.

All the godly ministries involved were grieved by the publicity concerning the Bakkers and the quarrels—because it tended to dry up the money that had come to them. The old hymn goes "Praise God from whom all blessings flow." But the TV preachers seemed equally interested in the true believers from whom all money flowed.

These evangelist broadcasters were all avowed Christians; some were fundamentalists, others "charismatic" ministers or something else. But in one respect they were all non-denominational—they were willing to accept money in any denominations.

Stay tuned.

"WE PRAY, OH LORD, FOR OUR BELOVED BROTHER IN CHRIST, WHO WE HOPE YOU WILL STRIKE DEAD IF HE TRIES TO MOVE IN ON THIS TERRITORY"

5/31/87

"THE LORD MOVES IN MYSTERIOUS WAYS"

3/24/87

"BLESS YOU — BLESS YOU TWENTY TIMES — BLESS YOU A HUNDRED TIMES — "

6/12/86

"IMAGINE THOSE ISLAMIC FUNDAMENTALISTS THINKING THEY HAVE THE REVEALED TRUTH!"

6/13/85

"'GRACIOUS, THOMAS,' SAID HUCKLEBERRY FINN TO HIS FRIEND, THOMAS SAWYER, 'SEE THE DOG, SPOT. SEE SPOT CHASE THE BALL.'"

"WE'RE LOOKING AFTER YOUR BEST INTERESTS"

Administration cuts in children's aid programs

Administration $734,371.22 study of Playboy, Penthouse and Hustler magazines

©1985 HERBLOCK
5/9/85

♪ "M—E—E—S—E" ♫

ANTI-VIDEO STORES

ANTI-SUPREME COURT

ANTI-PLAYBOY

MEESEKETEERS

©1986 HERBLOCK
10/24/86

OF COURSE, WE DISAPPROVE OF VIOLENCE, BUT WE UNDERSTAND THE FEELINGS OF PEOPLE WHOSE HONEST BLOOD IS STIRRED BY THE SLAUGHTER OF HELPLESS BABIES IN COLD-BLOODED, VICIOUS MURDERS

"PRO-LIFE" DEMAGOGUES

SUPREME COURT

FAMILY PLANNING AND ABORTION CLINICS

©1985 HERBLOCK
3/6/85

"WELCOME TO THE CLUB, JUNIOR"

I.R.A.

LIBYAN TERRORISTS

TERRORISTS AGAINST ABORTION AND FAMILY PLANNING CLINICS IN THE U.S.

IRANIAN TERRORISTS

©1984 HERBLOCK
11/30/84

"DON'T TELL ME THIS STUFF DOESN'T CAUSE VIOLENCE"

©1986 HERBLOCK
7/4/86

"AND WE PRAY THAT YOU SINNERS OUT THERE WILL SEE THE LIGHT"

"AHA, A 'LIBERAL ARTS' DEGREE! WHY NO FAR-RIGHT ARTS DEGREE? AND WHY <u>BACHELOR</u> OF ARTS? OBVIOUSLY ANTI-FAMILY"

©1985 HERBLOCK
12/11/85

"GUILTY OF NOT TEACHING RELIGION AND THEREFORE PRACTICING WITCHCRAFT"

©1987 HERBLOCK
3/8/87

"THAT TRIANGLE SUGGESTS A TRINITY. THAT STRAIGHT LINE DOESN'T EXPLAIN THE SHORTEST DISTANCE TO HEAVEN. THAT EQUAL SIGN SUGGESTS HUMANISM. AND WHY ARE YOU USING A MATH BOOK INSTEAD OF A BIBLE?"

©1986 HERBLOCK
10/30/86

"ON, CRUSADERS, AGAINST THE INFIDELS!"

©1985 HERBLOCK

8/9/85

KIDS OF ALL AGES!
NOW YOU CAN BUY THE OFFICIAL U.S. GOVT. SEX SHOP BOOK (or Meese Does Manhattan) NOT A SCIENTIFIC STUDY Just a book by guys who know what you should like.

TITILLATE YOURSELF WITH SOME REAL OFFBEAT DESCRIPTIONS

INCLUDES THE SEX STUFF DIGEST choice dialogue from x-rated movies

PLUS How to operate as a SEX VIGILANTE Learn how to be a censor! Intimidate your local stores!

ALL THIS AND MORE!

WRITE TO: Your Tax Dollars At Work, U.S. Dept. of Justice, Washington, D.C.

©1986 HERBLOCK

7/10/86

"UNCONVENTIONAL, BUT IT INVOLVES NO QUESTIONABLE METHODS"

CREATION

©1987 HERBLOCK

3/22/87

"HELP THE POOR? WHAT KIND OF RELIGION IS THAT?"

Put organized prayer in the public schools — Teach creationism — Moral Majority for more nukes

BISHOPS' LETTER

©1984 HERBLOCK

11/13/84

"HEY, WOW! LOOK AT THIS — I MEAN AIN'T IT AWFUL?"

MEESE PORNOGRAPHIC COMMISSION

©1986 HERBLOCK

5/28/86

In Performance

Among the many good programs brought to us by public television have been the musicales, hosted by presidents, called *In Performance at the White House*. These have been a pleasant diversion from official White House performances, which are less musical but more showy.

The performances of the Reagan administration not only have featured a glitz and an affinity for the camera that have reminded us of Hollywood; they have also recalled the titles of the stage spectaculars once produced by Florenz Ziegfeld and by George White—called, respectively, "the Follies" and "the Scandals."

In Performance at the White House Offices has included some light moments—or at least some lines that would have been considered funny if they had not been spoken by people in high positions. There was chief of staff Donald Regan, caught in a time warp when men were macho and women were home bodies. He said that women were "not going to understand [nuclear missile] throw-weights or what is happening in Afghanistan or what is happening in human rights." And in defending the administration's no-sanctions policy toward South Africa—which digs up diamonds and gold as well as apartheid policies—Regan asked, "Are the women of America prepared to give up all their jewelry?" With equal finesse he compared his job to that of a man in the shovel brigade that follows a parade down main street cleaning up afterward. At least one correspondent noted that many people regarded Regan as one of the elephants.

Edwin Meese, presidential confidant and attorney general, gave a passable imitation of W.C. Fields trying to maintain dignity while keeping two steps ahead of the sheriff. It was one of the great thoughts of this head of the Department of Justice that "You don't have many suspects who are innocent of a crime. That is contradictory. If a person is innocent of a crime, then he is not a suspect." After first claiming he was misquoted, it was one of Mr. Meese's great second thoughts that he had not meant what he said.

Caspar Weinberger, in the role of secretary of defense, appeared on almost any available broadcast to reel off a non-stop line of patter meant to explain why stamping "okay" on practically any order for military devices represented a policy.

Most of the administration performers had a penchant for props and a faith in gadgetry and trick solutions to problems. They liked lie detectors and routine drug tests and pushed for a presto-magic constitutional amendment to balance the budget; a Star Wars program to keep nuclear bombs from falling; and multi-billion-dollar plans to keep things humming if the bombs do land on us.

There was also a reliance on semantic gimmickry—a few well-chosen or well-twisted words to make a bad performance sound boffo. And where new words wouldn't do the trick, there were new *interpretations* of old words—so that the words in an ABM treaty or a constitutional ruling, or a Boland amendment or some other law didn't really mean what Congress, the courts and everyone had supposed them to mean.

Television made possible the triumph of audio-visual performance over performance on the job—switching the question from *What are they doing?* to *How did they come across?* Like most performers, the Reagan troupe did not like critical reviews. These troupers blamed their failures on the media—and they were adept at using the media to attack the media.

When he was head of intelligence operations, the late William J. Casey not only attacked the media for what they did but threatened newspapers and networks for what they *might* do. And when Adm. John Poindexter was national security adviser, he was responsible for the administration putting out what he called "disinformation"—intended to deceive Libya but that actually deceived Americans.

If a show title were selected for the Reagan White House performance, it would have to be *Anything Goes*. This would take in both the follies and the scandals, which resulted from an absence of ordinary government standards. In May 1987, *Time* magazine ran a cover story on ethics with pictures of some of the "more than 100 Reagan administration officials [who] have faced allegations of questionable activities."

Ronald Reagan had not only run against the federal government when he first campaigned for the presidency; he continued to run against it while heading it. So there might be considered a certain logic to his efforts to get around government rules and restrictions when they interfered with what he and his band of performers wanted to do.

November 1986 was not a happy time for that band. Despite Reagan's all-out campaign efforts, the Republicans lost the Senate. At the same time the foreign follies became major scandals. What was then in performance at the White House was Operation Damage Control.

NEW FIRST LINE OF DEFENSE

PASS, FRIEND

PATRIOTISM BY POLYGRAPH

©1985 HERBLOCK
7/5/85

"THE DAMN PRESS—REPORTING WHAT THOSE REPUBLICANS IN CONGRESS HAVE BEEN SAYING

©1986 HERBLOCK
12/2/86

"WHAT ARE YOU TRYING TO DO, MAKE ME LOOK BAD?"

CIA DIRECTOR Wm. J. Casey

HARBOR MINING

INTELLIGENCE FAILURES

PERSONAL FINANCIAL AFFAIRS

"MURDER MANUAL"

LATEST BUNGLE ON KGB AGENT

Senators

©1985 HERBLOCK
11/21/85

COMPETITIVENESS

Administration

©1987 HERBLOCK
2/5/87

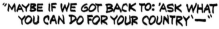

"MAYBE IF WE GOT BACK TO: 'ASK WHAT YOU CAN DO FOR YOUR COUNTRY'—"

6/6/85

"AND WE CAN SAY WITH PRIDE THAT WITH ALL THE SCANDALS AND SHADY DEALINGS IN OUR ADMINISTRATION, NOT ONE MEMBER HAS YET GONE TO JAIL"

10/28/84

"RIGHT, ED —THERE OUGHT TO BE SOME WAY YOU COULD PROSECUTE THOSE DAMN CIVIL RIGHTS LEADERS"

8/15/85

"DON'T WORRY ABOUT CONGRESS—YOU CAN LEAVE EVERYTHING IN MY HANDS"

8/23/85

"SOME OF YOU MIGHT ATTAIN HIGH PLACES IN GOVERNMENT, WHERE YOU CAN LINE UP SOME REALLY BIG-BUCK DEALS"

©1986 HERBLOCK

5/25/86

PRIZE CATCH • KGB AGENT

©1985 HERBLOCK
11/6/85

"DAMNED MEDIA!"

FOREIGN AGENTS WILL PLEASE TAKE A NUMBER

©1986 HERBLOCK
6/8/86

TO PRESERVE SECRECY WE OVERCLASSIFY LOTS MORE MATERIAL—REQUIRING LOTS MORE PEOPLE WITH SECURITY CLEARANCES—RESULTING IN MORE SPYING—SO—

©1985 HERBLOCK
6/7/85

"RIGHT, CHIEF—AS A MATTER OF FACT, I DON'T KNOW A SINGLE PERSON WHO'S GOING HUNGRY"

©1986 HERBLOCK
5/22/86

84

SPIRIT OF THE FOUNDING FATHERS
Administration version 1985

we mutually pledge to each other
our Lives, our Fortunes and our
~~sacred Honor~~ lie detector tests.

12/13/85

THE OVAL-TRACK ARMS RACE

7/13/86

"HEAR YE, HEAR YE — THIS COUNTRY WILL COME TO ORDER"

5/30/86

"THAT'S OUR BOY"

2/7/85

"PATIENCE"

2/10/85

"SOMEBODY CALL A DOCTOR — I MAY HAVE SPRAINED MY WRIST"

OIL PRICES

1973: $3-A-BARREL
1981: $35-A-BARREL
1986: $10-A-BARREL

OIL CONSUMERS

©1986 HERBLOCK
4/3/86

"MUCH ADO ABOUT NOTHING"
— Ronald Speakespeare

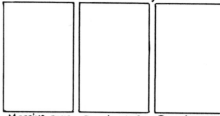

Massive arms supplies going from Nicaragua to El Salvador rebels.

Russian MIGs in Nicaragua.

Pages from CIA "murder manual" explaining that it's just a book of etiquette.

Low-level CIA aide responsible for the manual.

Explanations to contras that U.S. is not interested in overthrowing the government of Nicaragua.

Wonderful new "Emperor brand" clothes being woven by Administration tailors.

©1984 HERBLOCK
11/20/84

"THAT'S AN UNFAVORABLE BROADCAST — THAT NETWORK NEEDS TO BE NEUTRALIZED"

CIA
Wm. J. Casey
Director

ABC

W.J.C.

Handbook On How To Assassinate The U.S. Constitution

©1984 HERBLOCK
11/28/84

"SIR ISAAC NEWTON HE'S NOT"

FALLING OIL PRICES

DROP IN ESTIMATES OF FUTURE OIL SUPPLIES

FILL THE U.S. PETROLEUM RESERVE

RAISE GAS AND OIL TAXES

ADMINISTRATION

©1985 HERBLOCK
7/9/85

"FOUNDING FATHER, IF YOU APPROVE WHAT WE'RE DOING, RAP TWICE"
Attorney General
Dept. of Justice
©1985 HERBLOCK
10/27/85

MAÑANA REPUBLIC

8/24/86

3/17/87

THE BUCK STOPS THERE

2/17/85

"SO WHAT ARE PEOPLE SURPRISED ABOUT?"

4/4/86

THE OVER-ABUNDANT THANKSGIVING SEASON

©1985 HERBLOCK
11/27/85

"THE RUSSIANS WILL STOP AT NOTHING—NOW THEY'VE STOLEN OUR MOST IMPORTANT TECHNOLOGY"

©1985 HERBLOCK
10/8/85

"THEY DON'T HAVE SCANDALS ANY MORE— THEY CALL IT PRIVATIZATION OR SOMETHING"

©1986 HERBLOCK
6/11/86

"CHIEF, AT THE DISPLAY OF THE FLAG, IS THE HEART SUPPOSED TO BEAT TRUE OR SKIP A BEAT?"

"OHBOY—THOSE FOOLISH RUSSIANS"

NATIONAL SECURITY POLICY

"IT'S AWFUL THAT SO MANY PEOPLE AROUND THE PRESIDENT DID THESE THINGS — WHO IN THE WORLD HIRED THOSE PEOPLE?"

©1987 HERBLOCK

6/28/87

Names on a Small Globe

Reading the papers and watching TV may not be broadening in the same way as travel, but you cover the territory a lot faster.

"Faraway places with strange-sounding names" is a line in a song. But the places are no longer so far away and the names become less strange-sounding with repetition. Sri Lanka turns out to be old romantic-sounding Ceylon. I don't know when somebody decided that all Chinese names should now contain an X or a Z. But I guess I can adjust to that. Whatever the latest spelling of the name of Libya's leader, he's still Col. Qaddafi to me. I had a hard enough time learning to spell it *that* way. On changed spellings you have to draw the line somewhere.

Glasnost has been a welcome addition to the language and probably to most Russians—although ironically it seems to cause concern among East-bloc communist rulers who learned their trade the old way. Chernobyl is a name that sets off alarms throughout the world, as it should. Reykjavik and Bitburg have become not only names on correspondents' suitcases, but heavy presidential baggage. Names of African countries have been brought closer to home by the too-familiar face of hunger. And Contadora—a small Panamanian island where statesmen met—became a word of hope for peace in Latin America even when it remained just an island to the White House.

The Olympic Games may not create the international goodwill they're supposed to; but if the prospect of these games helps advance South Korea toward democracy, they're worth all the hoopla and commercialism that goes with them.

We like to see freedom on the go.

"THIS TIME I'M REALLY GOING TO GET THAT BLEEP-BLEEP ROADRUNNER"

5/19/85

12/20/84

10/26/84

"ANOTHER THING — I DON'T LIKE THEM CALLING US FERDINAND AND IMELDA"

3/16/86

"HE HAS TO—THERE WERE A COUPLE OF THINGS HE FORGOT TO STEAL"

"THOSE WERE THE GOOD OLD DAYS"

10/29/85

"ON THE OTHER HAND, IF WE CUT DOWN ON THEIR VODKA, THERE'S LIABLE TO BE A BIG INCREASE IN RUSSIAN ROULETTE"

6/9/85

"YOU CAN SEE WE'RE NOT A COMPLETELY CLOSED SOCIETY"

5/2/86

"AND NOW SOME MORE OFFICIAL INFORMATION ON THE ACCIDENT AT CHERNOBYL"

©1986 HERBLOCK
5/6/86

HARVEST IN ETHIOPIA

©1984 HERBLOCK
11/14/84

"JA — FOR A LEADER TO CHANGE PLANS WOULD SHOW WEAKNESS"

©1985 HERBLOCK

4/26/85

"— UNLIKE OUR GOVERNMENT, WHERE EVERYTHING WRONG IS THE FAULT OF SUBORDINATES"

"THE AWFUL EVIL STARTED BY ONE MAN..."

HISTORY REVISION I
Prof. Reagan

©1985 HERBLOCK

5/7/85

"OH, ALL RIGHT — I COULD ALSO THROW IN A SIDE TRIP FOR THE GUYS WHO WERE ON THE OTHER SIDE"

DIED
FOR THE THIRD REICH
IN THE WAR
TO END FREEDOM
EVERYWHERE

©1985 HERBLOCK

4/16/85

The Winds of Freedom

©1986 HERBLOCK

5/1/86

MARATHON MAN

©1986 Herblock
4/29/86

"NOW IT'S ACID BRAIN"

WHITE HOUSE PROTECTIONISM TO PREVENT CONGRESSIONAL PROTECTIONISM

©1986 HERBLOCK

6/4/86

"NONSENSE — I DON'T BELIEVE IN PEOPLE"

HOFDI HOUSE Reykjavik

©1986 HERBLOCK

10/7/86

"WELL, YOU PROTECTED YOURSELF BETTER THAN YOU PROTECTED US"

JURY FINDINGS IN SHARON LIBEL CASE

VICTIMS OF PALESTINIAN CAMP MASSACRES

©1985 HERBLOCK

1/25/85

"LET A THOUSAND FLOWERS BLOOM"

NUCLEAR PROLIFERATION

©1985 HERBLOCK

10/23/85

"SO I GOT UP FROM THAT TABLE WITH GORBACHEV AND WALKED OUT — AND YOU CAN IMAGINE MY SURPRISE WHEN I FOUND OUT WHAT WE HAD BEEN TALKING ABOUT"

©1986 HERBLOCK
10/28/86

"FOR US, THIS PAINFUL AFFAIR IS CLOSED" —Prime Minister Shamir

POLLARD CASE

SPY DATA

ISRAELI GOVT. OFFICIALS

©1987 HERBLOCK
3/10/87

"BUT I'M HAPPIEST ABOUT THE GRANDCHILDREN"

40 YEARS U.S.-U.S.S.R. 50,000 WARHEADS

MORE COUNTRIES WITH NUCLEAR POTENTIAL

©1985 HERBLOCK
8/7/85

"WE'D BETTER CALL CENTRAL CASTING AGAIN, CHIEF"

Founding Fathers For Nicaraguan Contras

BALONEY CLAIM OF PAPAL SUPPORT

©1985 HERBLOCK
4/19/85

"HOW DO YOU SCORE THIS GAME?"

U.S.

©1985 HERBLOCK
5/8/85

"THE CIVILIANS ARE GETTING OUT OF HAND"

PHILIPPINE COUP ATTEMPT

ARGENTINE MILITARY REVOLT

©1987 HERBLOCK
4/21/87

"YOU'VE HEARD OF WILBUR AND ORVILLE"

PLAN FOR NICARAGUA

JIM WRIGHT

DEM

©1987 HERBLOCK
8/7/87

VENETIAN SUNSET

WORLD LEADERSHIP

©1987 HERBLOCK
6/12/87

"IF THE RUSSIANS KEEP ON WITH LIBERALIZATION WE MAY HAVE TO SEND TANKS IN THERE"

STALIN

ROMANIA

CZECHO SLOVAKIA

EAST GERMANY

© 1987 HERBLOCK
7/31/87

©1987 HERBLOCK

6/30/87

Defense—Hah!

In the beginning was the Word—and it meant what it said. But words are not always that simple and straightforward. Some of them are downright deceptive. Take "national security." It is often a convenient cover for government bungles and misdeeds.

Or take "conservative." We used to have at least a ballpark idea of what a conservative was. But that term has now been stretched so far it has gone over the right-field wall to cover assorted kooks and radicals.

And then there's "defense," as in "defense spending." It doesn't seem like quite the right word for $7,000 coffeepots or $640 toilet seats; or worse, for untested and non-working weapons that we—and our troops—ought to be defended against.

In its haste to spend money the Pentagon even followed a policy of buy first and try afterward—pay now and test later.

The MX missile has been officially labeled The Peacekeeper. And any scheme, however ill-advised or impractical or even illegal, has become an "initiative." We not only have the Strategic Defense Initiative (better known as Star Wars), but in the Iran-contra scandal, we heard the arms-for-hostages deal referred to as "the Iran initiative"— something akin to the Titanic's "initial crossing."

In a number of cartoons I have shown the secretary of defense wearing the $640 toilet seat as a kind of collar. This not only represents the small items priced at a markup of several hundred percent, but it is symbolic of the billions of dollars that have been flushed down the drain in the name of defense.

Among notable Pentagon turkeys has been the DIVAD anti-aircraft gun, whose failure to function properly at last became too much even for the Pentagon. It was finally abandoned after an expenditure of $1.8 billion.

The B-1 bomber, killed off by the Carter administration because it was not a worthwhile aircraft and one that would soon be replaced by the Stealth bomber, was brought back to life by the Reagan administration, although perhaps in a brain-dead condition. Its flaws have required many thousands of design changes. Its high costs and repair bills keep increasing, along with its drawbacks. Its electronics are way off the beam, but the money for Pentagon contractors continues in steady flight.

The land-based MX missiles have had problems in addition to their long-time efforts to find suitable dwelling places. A June 1987 *Washington Post* article by Pentagon correspondent George C. Wilson reported:

> One-third of the 21 MX nuclear missiles cannot be fired for lack of guidance systems, the Air Force acknowledged yesterday as three civilian whistle-blowers warned Congress that the remaining MXs could not hit their targets because of shoddy workmanship. . . .

The Bradley "fighting vehicle" began as a troop carrier and became so loaded down with added weaponry and so vulnerable to enemy fire that it was not much good either for carrying troops or for fighting. The Bradley was supposed to be amphibious, but on entering water it has shown a tendency to roll to the bottom and stay there.

A troop-carrying vehicle that is likely to go up in flames when hit or to remain submerged when wet is not user-friendly. But under water it is at least harder to hit, and in some future version this hybrid might carry still fewer troops and become a carrier-fighting-vehicle-submarine.

Each add-on, designed to make every vehicle and plane a technological dreamboat, results in heavier costs as well as heavier loads. This means that fewer are affordable, even with record peacetime defense spending.

I have my own worst-case scenario about fewer-but-more-expensive-and-more-complicated fighting machines. In this nightmare, our country ends up with six super planes, costing a couple of trillion dollars each, incorporating everything that the minds of military men and contractors can devise, and designed to do anything on land, on sea or in the air. They find themselves facing an enemy fleet of a thousand low-cost, easy-to-operate planes. And while our pilots are trying to figure out which buttons to push to turn their planes into giant heat-resistant submersible coffeepots . . .

Never mind.

Whatever its failures in making wise provisions for national defense, the Pentagon has worked hard at defending itself. And its staunchest defender has been the commander in chief. When people became aware of the $435 hammers and $466 socket wrenches and $2,043 wing nuts, Mr. Reagan took to the airwaves to assert that these extravagances had actually been discovered and disclosed by his own watchful people. Not really. They were mostly discovered by Congress and by the independent inspectors general and testing executives that Congress had forced on a reluctant Reagan administration.

When stories appeared about $600 ashtrays on a plane, the Defense Department went into gear to appear to be doing something. Then-Secretary of the Navy John F. Lehman Jr. removed a rear admiral with 33 years' service and two lesser officers from their commands—despite the fact that the purchases had occurred before the admiral's tour of duty.

Secretary Weinberger announced the dismissals, citing them as evidence of the "very firm action" the Pentagon was taking against contractor overpricing. Some six weeks later the admiral was cleared and reinstated. The PR show was over.

This scapegoating "action" contrasts with Defense Department lack of necessary action. Evidence has shown that tests of the DIVAD missile launcher and of the Bradley vehicle were rigged to make these weapons appear to be safer and more capable than they actually were. DIVAD targets exploded without being hit. Firings at the Bradley were not aimed at its most vulnerable and inflammable sections.

Despite his defense of the Defense Department, Reagan finally appointed a commission, headed by David Packard, to study it and make recommendations. This commission indeed found things wrong, including purchasing and testing methods. Senators Barry Goldwater and Sam Nunn, both strong defense advocates, also came up with their own criticisms of the Pentagon. A committee that they headed was especially critical of interservice rivalries, which hampered military coordination. They also found a lack of combat-readiness. Goldwater cited waste and mismanagement and said of the Pentagon system, "It's broke and we need to fix it. It's clear the Department of Defense won't make the necessary changes."

Even without special commissions or the scrutiny of senators, it has been obvious that there has been something wrong with every recent combined service operation. That includes Desert One—the Carter

administration's hostage rescue mission in Iran—in which the participants seemed to be strangers to each other as well as to the environment.

In the Reagan team's invasion of Grenada, 3½ years later, casualties
were suffered and valuable time lost because communications were so
bad that the armed services literally were not on the same wavelength.
In a scene that might have come from the movie *Dr. Strangelove*, one
Army paratroop officer finally used his AT&T credit card on a civilian
phone to call Ft. Bragg, N.C., in the hope of getting the Army to
communicate with the Navy's ships off Grenada.

The bombing raids on Lebanon and Libya also were marked by
failures and lost lives.

In the July 1987 ''reflagging'' of ships in the Persian Gulf, the very
first Kuwaiti tanker flying the American flag was damaged when it hit
a mine. The secretary of defense explained that we ''did not look'' for
a mine in that particular location ''because there had never been any
mines in that area.''

Apparently our super-duper vastly increased Navy was a little short
on unglamorous items like minesweepers. With all the emphasis on
super weapons, perhaps we had become missile-bound.

Among recent events to give us thoughtful pause was the 1987 hit
on a U.S. warship, the Stark, by a missile fired from an Iraqi plane.
And still fresh in memory are the accidents in civilian nuclear plants
at Three Mile Island (U.S.A., 1979) and—more seriously—at Chernobyl (U.S.S.R., 1986).

All these things were not caused by sinister moles working within
intelligence systems or by gremlins. They were the result of human
error. And the malfunctioning machines sometimes try to show that
they are only human too.

The many military examples of Murphy's Law might be kept in mind
when we consider Star Wars. And we might also think about the little
Cessna plane, flown by a teen-age civilian from West Germany through
Russia's mighty defenses, to land in Moscow's Red Square.

By now nobody (except a few very young and impressionable kids
who believed the protective ''rainbow'' commercial on television)
thinks that Star Wars can provide a magic umbrella against evil spirits
—or an evil empire. But the program moves along on a carpet of cash
spread out across the country into many congressional districts and
research laboratories—and even abroad to our allies.

The Pentagon, with Star Wars in its eyes, every so often professes
to see a momentary breakthrough and talks about early deployment.
The one thing that seems certain to shoot up into space is the cost.

As a presidential candidate, Ronald Reagan called for an end to Waste, Fraud and Abuse in government and for a stronger national defense. Both of those objectives would serve well for his successor, who will find Waste, Fraud and Abuse right there in Pentagon contracting. We need to be protected on the home front as well as from foreign threats. When the Pentagon pushes on with costly but ineffective programs, it is cutting deep into home territory.

The call to Congress should be: Hold That Line!

DEEfense! DEEfense! DEEfense!

"I KNEW THAT DEFENSE BUDGET WOULD PUT US AHEAD OF THE RUSSIANS SOME WAY"

$1,075.00 bolt

$2,043.00 per nut

$7,600.00 COFFEE-BREWING MACHINE FOR C-5A CARGO PLANES

PENTAGON MALFUNCTIONING PLANES, TANKS, GUNS, MISSILES

©1984 HERBLOCK
9/23/84

SACRED BULL

PENTAGON SPENDING

DOMESTIC PROGRAMS

©1985 HERBLOCK
2/20/85

"WHAT DO THEY MEAN WE'RE NOT COMBAT-READY?"

ARMY

AIR FORCE

NAVY

GOLDWATER-NUNN REPORT

©1985 HERBLOCK
10/18/85

SOLDIER OF FORTUNE

CHARGE! AND OVERCHARGE

GEN. DYNAMICS

©1985 HERBLOCK
12/4/85

STRATEGIC DEFENSE

©1985 HERBLOCK.

5/1/85

"CROSS MY PALM WITH 30 BILLIONS OR SO FOR STARTERS"

MILITARY ASTROLOGY

STAR WARS

©1985 HERBLOCK
10/31/85

"LET'S HEAR IT FOR THIS AMAZING FEAT— SAWING A CORNER OF A BOX IN HALF"

PENTAGON OVERSPENDING

©1985 HERBLOCK
1/6/85

"IT TAKES A LOT MORE PEOPLE TO FIGURE WAYS TO SPEND ALL THAT MONEY"

BUILDING PROPOSAL FOR ADDING A "2nd PENTAGON"

©1986 HERBLOCK
8/3/86

"YOU AGAIN?"

HELP A HOMELESS MISSILE JUST A FEW BILLIONS MORE

CONGRESS

©1984 HERBLOCK
1/2/85

"YOU KNOW WHAT'S GREAT ABOUT AN UNLIMITED ARMS RACE? UNLIMITED ARMS SPENDING"

UP, UP, UP WITH STAR WARS

DOWN WITH SALT

©1986 HERBLOCK
6/20/86

"I'M NOT GOING TO STAY WITH A BOAT THAT HAS FLAWS IN IT"

STAR WARS

SALT II

©1986 HERBLOCK
6/5/86

"IT'S AN OLD TRADITION — THE ADMIRAL GOES DOWN WITH THE ASHTRAY"

LABORATORY EXPERIMENT

GOVT. FUNDS FOR RESEARCH

YES, I BELIEVE IN STAR WARS

SCIENCE

©1986 HERBLOCK
5/14/86

"I CAN QUIT ANY TIME I WANT TO"

CONGRESS

OLD MX

©1985 HERBLOCK
3/29/85

My daddy says nuclear missiles could hurt us

and even hurt our house, bringing down property values.

So daddy says we can build a rainbow around our house

and maybe the nuclear missiles will bounce off the rainbow

CONTRACT

My daddy works on Star Wars and says there's a pot of gold in that rainbow for us.

WE ♥ STAR WARS

BARF

©1985 HERBLOCK

My daddy is smart. He really knows how to turn a buck.

11/8/85

"IT'S THE OPPOSITE OF VOYAGER—— WE NEED CONSTANT REFUELING AND DON'T GET ANYWHERE"

"I THOUGHT MAYBE THE THREE OF US COULD, SORT OF, YOU KNOW..."

10/14/86

"MEN, WE ARE FACING A BATTLE TO PRESERVE OUR WAY OF LIFE"

5/12/85

PENTAGON REPORTS

THE BRADLEY TROOP CARRIER IS DOING FINE

THE B-1 DOESN'T HAVE ANY REAL PROBLEMS

THE DIVAD GUN SYSTEM LOOKED GOOD IN TESTS

AND WE'RE MAKING 'SIGNIFICANT PROGRESS' ON STAR WARS

4/29/87

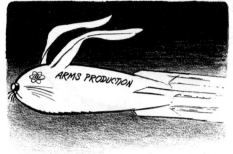

©1985 HERBLOCK
3/15/85

"OUR BAGS ARE PACKED"
— Weinberger on Star Wars program

©1987 HERBLOCK
1/25/87

"JUST WHEN WE WERE READY FOR LAUNCHING"

©1987 HERBLOCK
5/13/87

©1987 HERBLOCK
6/2/87

Constructive Enragement

In pursuing its racial policy of apartheid, the government of South Africa has been seen throughout the world to be violating human rights, and seen on television beating and shooting people in the streets. The government, under P.W. Botha, felt that something had to be done about this. It did not change its policies—it changed what people could see of those policies in action. It imposed strict censorship to prevent its violations of human rights from being shown on camera or reported. This white minority government even made it illegal for reporters to refer to it as a white minority government.

As the old question goes, when a tree falls in a forest, and no one is there to hear, does it make a noise? The South African government did indeed eliminate the noise—the sounds of blacks being clubbed; the cries of families whose loved ones were killed by the government; the cries for freedom and basic rights from within the country; the whir of cameras and the clack of typewriter keys reporting what went on. But the people continued to be felled even though we couldn't hear or see. In November 1985, 3½ weeks after the chromium curtain had been dropped around South Africa, we learned that in one week alone 33 more blacks had been killed—13 shot in a single day.

The Reagan administration's policy of "constructive engagement" appeared not to be constructive or to engage anyone in a way that protected human rights. Supporters of "engagement" argued that stronger steps to express American displeasure with South Africa could not bring that government to its knees. Probably not. But we could show that we were not on our knees before any dictatorship that professed to be anti-communist. We could send a message to its people and to others throughout the world that we found its racial practices and its violations of basic rights intolerable. We could at least, as Sen. Edward Kennedy expressed it, put ourselves "on the right side of history." And even an administration not sufficiently concerned about what went on inside South Africa might have shown real anger over that government's military forays into neighboring countries.

It seemed to me that during the total blackout—or whiteout—of news, it might have been a good idea for television stations regularly to run file footage of what had gone on and was still going on in that country. In the absence of active and colorful video tape, I'm including here some cartoons to serve as reminders.

"WE'LL TEACH YOU TO SAY THAT WE'RE NOT TREATING YOU BETTER"

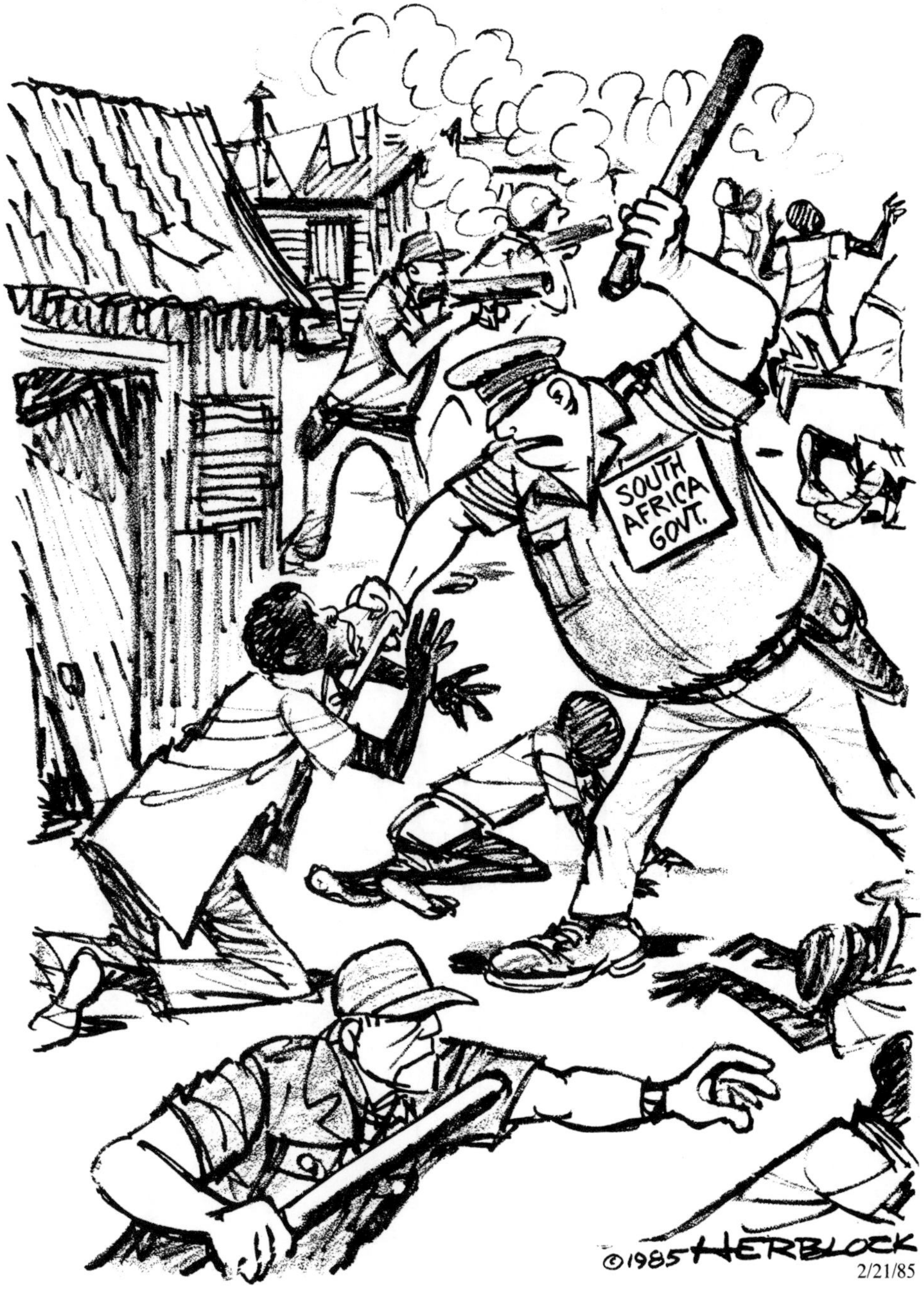

"WE'VE SHOWN THEM THAT NON-VIOLENCE DOESN'T WORK—NOW TO CONVINCE THEM THAT VIOLENCE IS NO GOOD"

BLACKS: NO REPRESENTATION NO RIGHTS NO CIVILIZED TREATMENT NO HOPE OF IMPROVEMENT

SOUTH AFRICA GOVT.

RIOTS BOMBINGS

©1984 HERBLOCK
9/5/84

PROGRESS

KILLED BY SOUTH AFRICAN GOVERNMENT IN MARCH, 1960 MASSACRE

KILLED BY SOUTH AFRICAN GOVERNMENT IN MARCH, 1985 MASSACRE

©1985 HERBLOCK
3/22/85

A PROCESS OF CHANGE IS UNDER WAY
—U.S. State Department

EVOLUTION TO CIVILIZED MAN

YOU ARE HERE X

SOUTH AFRICA GOVT.

©1984 HERBLOCK
12/5/84

"CONGRESS DOESN'T APPRECIATE WHAT A GOOD INFLUENCE I'VE HAD ON YOU"

SOUTH AFRICA GOVT.

©1986 HERBLOCK
10/1/86

"MR. AFFIRMATIVE REACTION HERE ——
DR. CONSTRUCTIVE ENGAGEMENT, I PRESUME"

8/22/85

THE EMERGENCY ORDER IS "TO ENSURE THAT A
NORMAL COMMUNITY LIFE IS REESTABLISHED"
—Botha

NORMAL COMMUNITY LIFE

7/23/85

MOVEMENT IN SOUTH AFRICA

8/16/85

ENDLESS PROCESSION

7/14/85

"THEY ARE DEAD AND THAT'S THAT"
— South African spokesman, responding to questions about shootings of blacks.

©1985 HERBLOCK
7/28/85

SELF-DIVESTITURE

©1986 HERBLOCK
5/23/86

"WE HAVE TO HANG ON TO CHANGE ITS DIRECTION"

©1986 HERBLOCK
6/22/86

Dear Ms. Lovelorn—
I am engaged to a South African gentleman who is, as my friends say, a monster. But I say, nobody's perfect, and I do not wish to break our engagement, which I feel is very constructive.

©1986 HERBLOCK
7/3/86

©1986 HERBLOCK
6/13/86

THE BEHAVIOR LESSON

Hear Ye! Hear Ye!

In this land of the free and home of the litigious, who has not heard the full-throated cry of the aggrieved: *I'll fight this all the way to the Supreme Court!* It is our secular Seat of Judgment, but it is not the Last Judgment—there is always another day, another opinion, when there might be another justice or two on the bench.

This thought has not escaped President Reagan or his attorney general, Edwin Meese—a committed ideologue who is about as far out as it's possible to get without being hauled off by National Archives building guards for taking an ax to the Constitution.

In a 1986 speech, Meese suggested that Supreme Court rulings are not the law of the land, and called it "astonishing" that the court's unanimous 1954 decision for school desegregation should apply to other states besides the one in which it was brought. Mr. Meese is pretty astonishing himself, and untiring in his efforts not only to repeal the rulings of the Warren court but to roll back the 20th century and part of the 19th. And what was wrong with that Dred Scott decision anyhow?

It is small wonder that Meese was unhappy with a court before which the Reagan administration agenda had only a modest batting average. In its policy of affirmative reaction, that administration managed, by reneging on a deal with Congress, to gain control of the Civil Rights Commission, which up until then had been an independent body. But in the Bob Jones University case, the administration failed to overturn established government policy of denying tax exemption to schools that discriminate against blacks. In other words, it couldn't get a tax exemption for schools that practice discrimination. It also did not fare very well in affirmative-action cases involving minority hiring. The Supreme Court supported these.

Other items on the Reagan-Meese "social issues" agenda were not notably successful either. The court did not support their efforts to put organized prayer in the public schools or to restrict the right to have abortions. The administration had somewhat better luck in curbing rights of suspects, but Meese and Reagan probably still wince when they see TV shows in which the cops tell suspects: "You have the right to remain silent. You have the right to . . ."

It is often said—and a little too often, for me—that you never know what a person will do once he or she puts on that Supreme Court robe. That is quite true, particularly in the case of justices named by presidents like Eisenhower and Kennedy, for whom changing the court was not a major interest. What needs to be said more frequently is that a president who is determined to change the direction of the court and has sufficient nominees confirmed has a good chance of accomplishing his objective.

Franklin Roosevelt changed the court's tilt against New Deal economic programs. Richard Nixon, even though a couple of his nominees were rejected, turned the court more toward his law-and-order bent; and Reagan has tried to make sure of the kinds of decisions his nominees would hand down by selecting sitting judges with proven track records. For those who say you never know, I will give good odds that Justices William Rehnquist and Antonin Scalia do not turn out to be Hugo Black and William Douglas in disguise.

When Chief Justice Warren Burger resigned, Reagan and Meese had in Associate Justice Rehnquist the ideal person for the job. Here was a man who, on the court itself, had shown a doctrinaire position unlikely to be altered by time. It was a masterful political stroke to send up the nomination of Rehnquist to be chief justice and Scalia for associate justice at the same time. Rehnquist, who under questioning showed the memory lapses that afflict so many Reagan appointees, took all the heat; and Scalia slid in without a dissenting vote in the Senate. This was the same Scalia that William Safire had described, in a 1985 column, as "the worst enemy of free speech in America today" —a view based on that judge's opinions in First Amendment cases. In one case Scalia joined in an opinion expressing the idea that a newspaper's reputation for hard-hitting investigative reporting could be considered evidence of malice. With a few more hard-hitting and soft-thinking justices like that, the First Amendment could go down for the count.

I am an enthusiastic supporter of Russell Baker's effort to end abuse of the word "brilliant." Where judicial nominations are concerned, it is applied to any judge who got good grades in school and who can whittle some peg on which to hang a bad decision. Speaking of a "brilliant" seeker of loopholes is something like talking about a "brilliant" safecracker. What is generally meant is something like "clever" or "crafty."

Nixon talked about wanting "strict constructionists" on the court, a theme echoed by Reagan and Meese. It is remarkable how these people, operating under the Constitution and celebrating its bicentennial, could miss out on simple words like "with the advice and consent of the Senate."

They tell us the president was elected and he can name who he wants. And that's right. The Senate was elected too, and it does not need to consent to anyone it doesn't want.

When President Reagan nominated Judge Robert Bork to the Supreme Court, he said he hoped politics would not enter into the confirmation process, and he must have been biting his tongue to keep from laughing. Politics is what he built into his nominations. It's been estimated that by the time Reagan leaves office, he will have appointed half the federal judges in the United States. Quite a political legacy.

When a president and Congress are in a confrontational mode, where do they take their fight? All the way to the Supreme Court.

As long as there are five justices on that court who believe in the First Amendment, we can all chime in with our majority and minority opinions. As the clerk intones when the justices are seated: "God save this honorable court!" And all us just plain citizens too.

"THEY'RE FIRM SUPPORTERS OF THE CONSTITUTION — IT'S JUST SOME OF THE AMENDMENTS THEY DON'T LIKE"

REHNQUIST

SCALIA

©1986 HERBLOCK
8/22/86

HIGHER LAW

ANTI-ABORTION FANATICS

TERRORISTS

©1985 HERBLOCK
1/10/85

"THE NEWS BLACKOUT IN SOUTH AFRICA HAS BEEN ALMOST TOTAL... PRESS AND TV PEOPLE HAVE BEEN BANNED, CENSORED, EXPELLED..."

COURT NOMINEES RECORDS ON FIRST AMENDMENT CASES

THREATS TO PROSECUTE PRESS

Meese

Casey

©1986 HERBLOCK
6/19/86

"THE ONES AT THE BOTTOM ARE AWFULLY FAR GONE"

5/9/86

THE PRIZE

7/24/86

"AND, ABOVE ALL, DON'T COMPARE OUR WORTH WITH THAT OF AN ACTUAL CIVIL RIGHTS COMMISSION"

4/12/85

"HUP, TWO, THREE, FOUR——"

11/15/85

"WE'VE GOT TO BE COLORBLIND"

CITIES
AFFIRMATIVE ACTION PROGRAMS

REAGAN DEPT. OF JUSTICE

©1985 HERBLOCK
5/23/85

"SOMETIMES HE FORGETS–LITTLE THINGS LIKE THE PROPERTY COVENANT, HIS MEMO ON SEGREGATION, HIS ACTIVITIES IN ARIZONA, HIS PREVIOUS STATEMENTS, HIS RECORD, THE CONSTITUTION..."

©1986 HERBLOCK

8/6/86

©1987 HERBLOCK

7/7/87

©1986 HERBLOCK

6/27/86

"YOU WERE EXPECTING MAYBE EDWARD M. KENNEDY?"

©1987 HERBLOCK

7/2/87

"SO, AS YOU CAN SEE, YOU DON'T NEED TO BE CONCERNED ABOUT PRESIDENTIAL SELECTIONS FOR THE COURT"

10/21/84

"SAY, NOW THAT THE COURT HAS APPROVED PREVENTIVE DETENTION ——"

6/5/87

"YOU GOT SOME TICKETS YOU WANT FIXED? YOU HAVING PROBLEMS WITH THE HEALTH INSPECTOR? YOU GOT A SISTER IN TROUBLE? YOU NEED DOUGH?"

7/16/86

Just Politics

Will Rogers said it: "Politics has got so expensive that it takes lots of money to even get beat with." He said that at a time when a few thousand dollars was a lot of money. And "slush funds" were viewed as so scandalous that in 1929, the U.S. Senate refused to seat two men who had won elections using such funds—Frank L. Smith of Illinois and William S. Vare of Pennsylvania. The hundreds of thousands of dollars involved then were indeed scandalous, but in populous states like those they would not be enough to buy a Senate nomination today. And they might not even make a down payment on a Senate seat. In the 1986 elections, the *average* amount spent to win a Senate seat was $3 million.

Candidates and issues come and go, but the one political constant is money—and the ante has been raised by the more recent political necessity, television. Remarkably, in 1987 a majority of senators favored legislation to limit Senate campaign spending by providing some public financing. This ran into a filibuster led by Sen. Robert Dole. The filibusterers, who spend billions of taxpayers' money on home-state projects, expressed shock that some political campaigns might be conducted at public expense. Translation: they liked the system as it was and thought they had a spending advantage that way.

Hypocrisy is only one identifiable ingredient in political campaigns. We get quite a variety for our money—or the money of special-interest contributors. Where gun controls are an issue, the euphemistically titled National Rifle Association (NRA) weighs in with big money to make sure that cheap handguns, machine guns and other firearms are made available to as many people as possible as quickly as possible.

Most law-enforcement officers oppose the NRA position but do not have the large financial resources of the gun lobby.

Religion now mixes regularly with politics. The abortion issue is there too. And drugs. During the 1986 campaigns, when political drug-mania may have been at its peak, some candidates even challenged their opponents to urine tests—making literal the expression formerly used to describe low-level contests. Sometimes sex is there to spice things up. In the case of Gary Hart's presidential campaign, this long-distance front-runner tripped and fell on his own doorstep when it turned out that he had been terminally indiscreet.

The political season never ends and the running never stops. Election predictions are followed by election explanations and interpretations. Reagan supporters cited his landslide elections as a mandate for the other branches of government to fold up and go along with whatever he wanted on any issue. But when his all-out 1986 campaign for Republican candidates brought only a surprisingly decisive Democratic victory in the Senate, the new rationale was that the elections to the House and Senate somehow didn't express the popular will in the same way.

Our political campaigns, even with the elephant-and-donkey animal acts playing a diminished role, may be the greatest show on earth. As the saying used to go: You pays your money and you takes your choice.

You better choose because in one way or another you pay anyhow.

147

DAILY DEBATER

PAC CAMPAIGN FUNDS

9/26/84

"HAVE SOME MORE — IT'S GOOD FOR YOU"

8/30/84

"YOU THINK HIS ADMINISTRATION HAS BEEN BAD,
HIS DOMESTIC POLICIES ARE NO GOOD, YOU CAN'T
BELIEVE WHAT HE SAYS, HE MIGHT GET US INTO WAR
AND YOU'RE GOING TO VOTE FOR HIM — RIGHT?"

10/2/84

"A SERIES OF DEBATES WOULD BORE YOU"

9/11/84

"DON'T YOU REMEMBER, HON? IT WAS WHILE WE WERE ALL DRINKING CHAMPAGNE AT YOUR VICTORY PARTY"

3/26/86

"DON'T KNOCK 'EM — THEY'RE MAKING US LOOK LIKE REG'LAR FELLERS"

4/10/86

"I DON'T THINK WE'RE GONNA MAKE IT ANOTHER FOUR"

1/31/85

"RIGHT UP MY ALLEY"

7/19/85

1986 POLITICAL RACES

$

©1986 HERBLOCK
7/27/86

"GOLLY, THEY JUST COULDN'T HAVE BEEN MORE GOOD-NATURED — THEY LAUGHED A GREAT DEAL"

PLEASE
RAISE THE
PRICE OF
OIL
AGAIN

GROVELING
GEORGE
Have kneepads,
will travel

Saudi
Arabia

©1986 HERBLOCK
4/6/86

"EASY NOW — I THINK YOU'RE OVER THE WORST"

POLITICAL
DRUGMANIA

CALL OUT
THE ARMY

OLD
SPARKY

DRUG NET
TESTS FOR
EVERYONE

©1986 HERBLOCK
10/4/86

"SORRY, THEY'RE ALL IN THE BATHROOM"

THE
DRUG
PROBLEM

ADMINISTRATION
OFFICIALS
TESTING
PROGRAM

©1986 HERBLOCK
8/15/86

"MY NAME IS JOE CANDIDATE. MY OPPONENT IS A CROOK AND A SLEAZEBAG AND WOULD SELL YOUR DAUGHTERS INTO PROSTITUTION. THANK YOU." "PAID FOR BY THE JOE CANDIDATE COMMITTEE FOR CLEAN POLITICS."

"DON'T FORGET THAT IN 1984 REAGAN WAS ELECTED ABSOLUTE MONARCH"

"HOW ABOUT TURNING IT OFF UNTIL THE POLITICAL CAMPAIGNS ARE OVER?"

"HOW ABOUT THE ICELAND PLOY — WE ALL GO ON TV AND SAY IT WAS A GREAT SUCCESS"

"THAT'S MY BOY"

"GOSH — WHO WAS THAT MASKED MAN?"

CONGRESSIONAL PAY RAISE TO CONGRESS

clippety clop clippety clop clippety clop

© 1987 HERBLOCK
2/6/87

"LOOK AT THAT GUY GO"

CREDIBILITY GULCH

IRAN-CONTRA

RONALD DIDN'T-KNOW ANYTHING

GARY DIDN'T-DO-ANYTHING

© 1987 HERBLOCK
5/8/87

SPECIAL LINCOLN-AND-WASHINGTON BIRTHDAY SALE

Chairman Of Senate Finance Committee Invites Lobbyists To Breakfasts For $10,000.00 Apiece

© 1987 HERBLOCK
2/4/87

"IT'S MAYOR BARRY! HE CAME ALL THE WAY FROM CALIFORNIA TO FLY OVER OUR CITY"

MAIN THOROUGH-FARE DISASTER ROUTE #12

Washington D.C. 1987 A Capital Offense

© 1987 HERBLOCK
1/29/87

CAPITOL INVESTMENT

$

BIG CONTRIBUTIONS TO
KEY COMMITTEE MEMBERS

©1987 HERBLOCK
2/26/87

"IF CONGRESS GOES ALONG WITH US ON DECONTROLLING GUN SALES —"

©1985 HERBLOCK
12/10/85

"I ONLY COUNT 85"

©1987 HERBLOCK
4/19/87

"THERE HAS TO BE A BETTER WAY TO GET THERE"

©1987 HERBLOCK
5/26/87

THE RETURN TO TARA

THE ONCE SOLID SOUTH

©1987 HERBLOCK
2/11/87

"DID ANYONE GET THE LICENSE NUMBER?"

SENATE GOP FILIBUSTER

PUBLIC FINANCING OF CONGRESSIONAL CAMPAIGNS

©1987 HERBLOCK
6/14/87

"WHY CAN'T THEY PUT ON A RE-RUN OF MY FIRST TERM?"

©1987 HERBLOCK
8/6/87

"YOU KNOW WHAT BOTHERS ME? NOT BEING ABLE TO BELIEVE _OUR_ GOVERNMENT _EITHER_"

©1986 HERBLOCK
3/28/86

Tangled Web

Looking back on his single term in office, President Jimmy Carter said that the hostages had almost become an obsession with him. President Reagan profited politically but learned nothing from that. With him the hostages became an obsession too—but it was not his only one. He also had an obsession with secrecy and an obsession with fighting the government of Nicaragua. In addition, he had at least a strong penchant for, if not an obsession with, arms. All of these combined to produce the scandal of arms sales to Iran and the diversion of money from those sales—the *contra* connection. One other ingredient might be added to this witch's brew—Reagan's chronic carelessness with the truth. And like Shakespeare's witches, the participants in the scandal in effect chanted: "Fair is foul and foul is fair."

In the Great Deception, the United States government, while lecturing its allies against selling arms to Iran and urging a policy of no dealings with and no concessions to terrorists, secretly sold weapons to Iran in arms-for-hostages deals. Moreover, more new hostages were seized than the number of hostages released. Not only was our government revealed to have been duplicitous, but it had also played the fool to the government of the Ayatollah Ruhollah Khomeini. The leader of the free world had no clothes on.

Later revelations about the diversion of Iranian funds and the administration's backdoor support of the Nicaraguan contras were shocking, but nothing topped the initial impact of the disclosure of the secret shipments to our declared enemy.

The unraveling started on Oct. 5, 1986, when a plane carrying cargo to the contras was shot down over Nicaragua and an American, Eugene Hasenfus, was captured. The U.S. government's denial of any connection with the flight turned out to be false.

In November, news of the arms sale to Iran came out. An Iranian official then revealed that former national security adviser Robert C. McFarlane and four other Americans, carrying Irish passports, had traveled to Iran on a secret mission. It developed that they had brought along some pistols for their hosts, as well as a cake symbolically baked in the shape of a key. The cake, according to McFarlane, was the idea of Lt. Col. Oliver North, of the National Security Council (NSC) staff. On one meeting with Iranians in Europe, North had brought them a Bible containing a scriptural quotation written and signed by President Reagan. On an earlier trip he had taken along arms-dealer Albert Hakim disguised in a wig and a pair of fake eyeglasses. They used code names for themselves and all the persons and places involved. Tom Sawyer would have been happy to play with these boys, although he might have led them to adventures less disastrous.

On Nov. 13, Reagan made a speech, shot through with misstatements. He said, "We did not, repeat not, trade weapons or anything else for hostages." This was only a short time after an arms shipment had been exchanged for a hostage.

Less than a week later, he held a news conference, at which he said:

(A) Everything that we sold them could be put in one cargo plane and there would be plenty of room left over.

(B) We did not condone, and do not condone, the shipment of arms from other countries.

(C) These [TOW missiles] are a purely defensive weapon. It is a shoulder-carried weapon.

(D) We . . . have had nothing to do with other countries on their shipments of arms.

(E) [In answer to a question on whether there were no arms shipments but one or two after January 1986] That's right . . .

All of these statements were false.

In addition, his declaration that "we are going to observe that embargo [on arms to Iran]" was misleading.

On Nov. 25, President Reagan presented Attorney General Edwin Meese to a news conference, where Meese disclosed the Iran-contra diversion. During this conference, Meese also made statements that proved to be untrue.

At the end of November, President Reagan appointed a commission, headed by former Republican Sen. John Tower, to investigate the Iran-contra scandal.

In January 1987, Reagan told the Tower Commission that he did not know the NSC staff was engaged in helping the contras. Later he said he had "no detailed knowledge" of efforts to raise military aid. Still later he said, "There's no question about my being informed. . . . As a matter of fact, I was very definitely involved in decisions about support to the freedom fighters. It was my idea to begin with." His final rationale was that the congressional restrictions on aid did not apply to him or the NSC staff—all this from a president who accused Congress of vacillating.

Reagan also told the Tower Commission that he did not recall the November 1985 shipment of Hawk missile parts through Israel to Iran, which very possibly violated U.S. law. But according to testimony by Secretary of State George Shultz, Reagan had told him in a private conversation that he did know of the shipment.

The entire Iran-contra scandal disclosed a web of lies involving all who took part in the deals, including the president, national security advisers and staff members, the head of Central Intelligence and at least one cabinet member. They lied to Congress. They lied to the American people. In some cases they lied to each other or withheld facts from each other. President Reagan kept vital information from his secretary of state, secretary of defense and chief of staff, as well as from Congress. According to North, who readily acknowledged lying to Congress, CIA Director William J. Casey even told him to keep information from the CIA. There were deceptions within deceptions—and within the secret government itself a plan to create an independent free-wheeling "secret CIA."

For people obsessed with secrecy, nothing is ever secret enough—certainly not a government operating under the Constitution and laws of the United States.

Televised hearings by a joint House-Senate investigating committee began in early May 1987 and went on into August. A few snapshots come to mind: the way in which the various people involved in the scandal protected the president and praised each other—even when contradicting each other . . . the contemptuous attitude of former Maj. Gen. Richard Secord toward the committee—and the later testimony of others who asserted that in their arms sales, Secord and his partner Hakim mixed a strong sense of profit with their oft-stated patriotism . . . the revelation that out of some $16.7 million raised from the arms sales, only about $3.5 million got to the contras, who were supposedly in desperate condition.

There was the testimony of McFarlane that if he'd had the guts (his words) to tell the president what was wrong with his policy in Central America, he was afraid that CIA Director Casey or Defense Secretary Caspar Weinberger or U.N. Ambassador Jeane Kirkpatrick "would have said I was some kind of commie."

There was the disclosure that Iranian nationals had been privately shown through the White House, including the Oval Office, and the top-secret Situation Room; and that people with no security clearances had been shown classified documents—this by a lieutenant colonel who was fearful of giving information to a few authorized members of Congress.

There was the matter of presidential directives or "findings," necessary to initiate covert operations. In at least one case a finding authorizing a straight arms-for-hostages swap was retroactive, according to Adm. John Poindexter, who said he later destroyed it to save the president political embarrassment. President Reagan said he did not remember this arms-for-hostages finding. McFarlane referred to an earlier "mental" finding. One commentator observed that such findings seemed more like hidings.

The committee followed witnesses down Loss-Of-Memory Lane, which branches off from Down-The-Garden Path. North could remember with certainty things that the committee had already discovered and some that could not be proved, such as a purported bribe offer. But in other matters, including his conversations with Attorney General Meese, his powers of recall failed.

Poindexter's memory, reputed to have been "photographic," failed him constantly. Under questioning, there were 184 times when he couldn't recall or didn't remember. His memory also differed from North's. North told of at least five memos he had given Poindexter to be relayed to the president for approval of arms to Iran and diversion of part of the profits to the contras. Poindexter said of these memos, "I frankly don't think they existed."

McFarlane, whose memory also differed from North's on key points, cited his long-standing opinion that the NSC staff was covered by the Boland amendment restricting contra aid. President Reagan and other officials who did not question "Boland" at the time later claimed that it did not apply to them.

People who did not suffer loss of memory could recall President Richard Nixon's advice to his co-conspirators during an earlier investigation: "You can say, 'I don't remember.' You can say, 'I can't recall. I can't give any answer to that, that I can recall.' "

As far as viewers were concerned, the two witnesses who raised the

TV ratings were North and his secretary, Fawn Hall. Ms. Hall testified first, acknowledging her part and North's in the altering and shredding of documents. She also told of stuffing documents in her clothing so that she and North could smuggle them past the White House guards. She said that "sometimes you have to go above the written law." She also advanced the novel idea that every citizen is entitled to immunity. She expressed her total admiration for "every secretary's 'dream of a boss.' " North had previously received quite a buildup from arms-dealer Hakim, who expressed his love for North, and from Robert Owen, who described himself as a North "foot soldier," and who concluded his testimony by reading a poem about North.

North himself became the star of the proceedings. For his appearances, he wore his Marine uniform with full decorations, even though he had not worn it as an NSC staff member.

His performance was a tour de force, and his lawyer played a strong supporting role, with many speaking lines of his own.

Then came the Ollie phenomenon or Olliemania—the unleashed desire of many people for a strong and confident man who claimed he would get things done and never mind how. We had seen Ollies before under different names.

North was practiced not only in deception but at giving the impression of candor and openness. He admitted lying to Congress. He said he gave Congress responses that were "erroneous, misleading, evasive and false." He admitted destroying evidence, doctoring documents, backdating papers and helping to prepare a false chronology of events. North also acknowledged accepting a gift that he tried to cover up with phony letters. The gift of a home security system was necessary, he explained, but he regarded the cover-up of it as his one mistake.

As for the rest, he boasted of what he had done. At one point he said that he was shredding documents even while Department of Justice investigators were in his office. A good deal of shredding had already been done before Attorney General Meese began his slow-motion in-house investigation.

North's defense was a vigorous offense; he acted as if there was nothing to defend. He attacked Congress. He attacked and lectured the committee. He claimed he had done nothing wrong or illegal. Whatever he had done was in a cause that made it Right. Congress was Wrong. The press was Wrong. He said of his activities, "I didn't want to show Congress a single word on the whole thing." A covert operation made lying and destroying evidence and whatever else was necessary all right.

A line that might have provoked laughter if the committee was in a mood for laughing was North's statement that "lying does not come easy to me." The committee, fearful of appearing to be harsh, gave him full rein to make speeches. In these speeches, he made himself out to be a true patriot, overcoming all obstacles to help what he called the "freedom fighters."

The North style of earnest and folksy demagogy included some interesting touches. He spoke of asking "my best friend" about something, and it turned out that he was referring to his wife—and, by the way, he had been faithful to her for all these years—and then there was his little daughter, three of them in fact . . . and so on until another speech about how the Vietnam War had been lost on the home front and Congress was to blame for everything—and the Iran-contra deals were really a great success, until there were leaks or something. As North told it, all of his operations, including his worst failures, were glowing successes. And he sounded as if he believed it all himself.

He went over big on television, and as far as tough questioning was concerned, he was home free. The committee, which had originally given in to special demands by North's lawyer, ended up in disarray with several members making speeches affirming their own patriotism.

There was a postscript to the North testimony—not headline-grabbing but revealing. North had given two prime examples of leaks by members of Congress. In the first he told of a couple of senators who, North said, had come from a White House briefing about an imminent raid on Libya and had dashed to the nearest microphones to reveal information that had alerted the Libyans and probably caused the deaths of two fliers. Senate committee chairman Daniel Inouye had researched the matter and gave the facts: The two senators had not rushed to microphones or revealed anything when interviewed. *However,* the Executive Branch was responsible for a long list of broadcast and printed stories, which for weeks, days and hours before the Libyan attack, told what the U.S. was going to do and when—and even pinpointed where we would do it.

North's other example of a dangerous leak by congressmen involved the interception of the terrorists who hijacked the Achille Lauro cruise ship. This leak, to *Newsweek* magazine, had not come from congressmen either. It had come from Lt. Col. Oliver North.

These didn't affect the hearings but they told much about North—a zealot who, even while testifying under oath, would put out a total fabrication if he felt it would reflect badly on Congress, justify his actions and advance the cause of his leader.

The next witness was Adm. Poindexter. He shared North's contempt for Congress and showed a similar feeling for the press. Poindexter had not only been responsible for the "disinformation" campaign about Libya but also for misrepresentation about our invasion of Grenada. Even while this action was in progress and known to the Cubans, Poindexter, by misleading the White House press secretary, was responsible for the press being told that such an invasion was "preposterous."

At the hearings, his views on our government processes were summed up in his statement that he did not want any "outside interference." Poindexter said that he had authorized the contra diversion without consulting the president. Saying that "the buck stops with me," he claimed that he had given the president "deniability." Reagan supporters who had tried to make the entire investigation hinge on the need for a "smoking gun" were delighted to take the word of a smoking Poindexter.

After the theatrical appearance of North and the frequent fulminations of the North and Poindexter lawyers, it would seem that anything else must be anti-climactic. But truth is stranger than fiction. And when Secretary of State George Shultz came before the committee, his blunt and to-the-point statements were refreshing and even astonishing. He had no lawyer sitting next to him constantly whispering in his ear, and he had no trouble with his memory.

Shultz, who had opposed the arms-to-Iran policy, told of the administration infighting and backstabbing, in which he was cut off from information on important matters, particularly by Poindexter and Casey. He told of agreements with Casey, soon violated, while Casey privately recommended that Reagan fire Shultz. He told of Reagan "findings" known to the NSC staff but not to the secretary of state. He told of how at one session with the president, he gave his opinions "with the bark off" about public misstatements from the Oval Office. He even told of his humiliation in being denied a travel plane by one White House operative. Shultz described the Iran arms deals as "pathetic" and "crazy," and said that the people who conducted them "were taken to the cleaners." Hearing his straight statements was like sitting down to meat and potatoes after being locked inside a fudge factory.

The next witness was Edwin Meese, the administration's investigator of Iran-contra, whose inquiry was marked by a lack of curiosity and a lack of record-keeping. His cursory and friendly interviews with key figures were conducted alone and with no note-taking. His precautions in preventing destruction of records were next to nil. But he stuck to his original story that he had been engaged in a real fact-finding mission.

Sen. George Mitchell inquired about a key meeting at which Meese showed North a memo that related to the diversion of funds. Following that meeting North did a great deal of paper-shredding. Meese said, "We don't know whether those were relevant documents, irrelevant documents, or what they were."

Mitchell asked, "Do you think Colonel North spent from 11 o'clock in the evening until 4:15 the next morning, destroying irrelevant documents?"

Meese replied, "I think he probably did . . ."

Sen. Mitchell said of the performance of the nation's chief law-enforcement officer, "It's just very hard to accept."

Donald T. Regan testified to his limited knowledge of what went on when he was chief of staff.

Secretary of Defense Weinberger, along with Shultz, had strongly opposed the sale of arms to Iran. Of the original plan for negotiating with "moderates" in Iran, Weinberger noted: "This is almost too absurd to comment on." He learned of the actual deals from Defense Department intelligence gained from foreign sources. He also learned that the White House had ordered Defense's own National Security Agency to withhold further information from the secretary of defense.

One of the reasons many people sympathized with North and earlier witnesses may have been because they felt for the lonely individual facing a bank of congressmen and counsels. But this was not quite the case. In addition to the voluble lawyers of North and Poindexter, witnesses had on their side many highly vocal committee members. Sen. Orrin Hatch and Rep. Henry Hyde, among several others, were in there pitching for these witnesses all the time, even interrupting other committee members to do so.

Some of these right-wing committee members who were ready to acclaim North a hero were the toughest on Shultz. But most members liked what he had to say.

Of the other committee members, two are particularly worth quoting here. In the course of the hearings, Chairman Lee Hamilton of the House committee said:

> . . . These committees have heard some of the most extraordinary testimony ever given to the United States Congress. . . . A few things that stand out in my mind:
> An elaborate private network was set up to carry out the foreign policy. . . . Private citizens, many with divided loyalties and profit motives, sold arms and negotiated for the release of American hostages . . .

were given top-secret codes and encryption devices and had access to Swiss bank accounts used for United States covert actions and operations. The president was involved in private and third-country fundraising for the contras. Wealthy private contributors were courted at the White House, solicited in coordination with government officials and given what they were told was secret information. American policy became dependent on the contributions of private individuals and third countries.

The president approved the payment of . . . [funds] to terrorists to secure the release of hostages. Senior officials did not know and chose not to know important facts about policy.

A national security adviser and an assistant secretary of state withheld information and did not tell the Congress the truth concerning U.S. involvement in the contra supply operation and the solicitation of funds from third countries.

When official involvement with the contras was prohibited, officials of the National Security Council raised money, helped procure arms and set up a private network to ship arms to the contras. A United States ambassador negotiated an agreement with Costa Rica for a secret airstrip, and a CIA agent facilitated supply flights.

What these committees have heard is a depressing story . . . of not telling the truth to the Congress and to the American people . . . about remarkable confusion in the processes of government. Those involved, whether public officials or private citizens, had no doubt they were acting on the authority of the president. . . . For me, these events raise several questions and concerns.

First. Our government cannot function cloaked in secrecy. It cannot function unless officials tell the truth. The Constitution only works when the two branches of government trust one another and cooperate. Policy failed here because the processes of government failed. . . .

Second. Privatization of foreign policy is a prescription for confusion and failure. . . . Use of private parties to carry out the high purposes of government makes us the subject of puzzlement and ridicule.

Third. Accountability, including personal responsibility, has been absent. . . .

Accountability requires supervision and acceptance of responsibility up the chain of command . . . rigorous oversight by the Congress and a full exercise of the process of checks and balances . . . above all, the operation of the normal processes of government. . . .

In hearings sprinkled with enough quotations to fill an anthology, Chairman Hamilton gave one of the shortest and best from Thomas Jefferson: "The whole art of government consists in the art of being honest."

Sen. William Cohen said, in part:

. . . What does it mean, for example, when our government believes it must act in the shadows, using code words and whispers and foreign capital and Swiss bank accounts and profiteers and mercenaries, to carry out its objectives. How we conduct the nation's business is as crucial as why we're conducting it, because our motives may be high but the tactics might be low or lawless. And the means, for me at least, are more important than the motives. . . .

But what is of equal concern to me is how misrepresentations, crucial omissions and deliberate deceptions have been encouraged to masquerade as truths before congressional committees. Since last December, I have been dismayed to listen to a string of witnesses who suffer from either accommodating amnesia, bland indifference or deliberate ignorance about a program of fundamental importance to this administration. . . .

The questions about what the president knew and when he knew it did not have the same relevance they had in Watergate. Reagan, who wanted the hostage deal and who wanted aid to the contras by any means, obviously knew much more than he first let on. Like the Sherlock Holmes story in which the clue was the dog that didn't bark, what was missing, as the story unfolded, was a single moment when the president asked any questions or even once expressed shock at what happened. His only reaction was to make continued growls at Congress and at the investigation.

It was Reagan's administration. The people who engaged in deceptive and illegal activities were following his policies. It was his anti-government attitude, his contempt for Congress, his love of secrecy and military operations that they adopted. With his tolerance and encouragement of what people around him could do for private gain or presidential policy, the atmosphere was right for lawlessness in the same way that certain temperatures and environments are conducive to germ culture.

He had created the climate that made scandal possible, even inevitable.

"IT'S LIKE THE STRATEGY THAT WORKED SO WELL IN LEBANON"

CONGRESS

NICARAGUA

6/14/85

"GEE, AN OFFICIAL HYSTERICAL MARKER"

HARLINGEN, TEXAS
HERE, IN 1986, THE REAGAN ADMINISTRATION LOCATED THE NICARAGUAN RED TIDE BEFORE MOVING IT TO SAN DIEGO

3//14/86

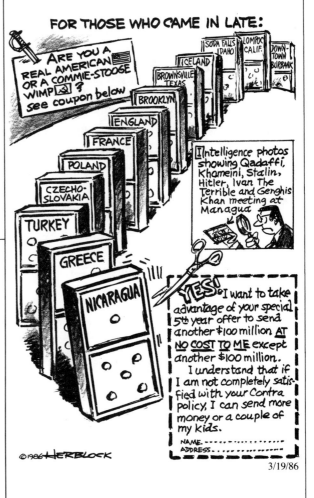

FOR THOSE WHO CAME IN LATE:

ARE YOU A REAL AMERICAN OR A COMMIE-STOOGE WIMP? see coupon below

BROWNSVILLE TEXAS
ICELAND
SODA FALLS IDAHO
LOMPOC CALIF.
DOWNTOWN BURBANK

BROOKLYN
ENGLAND
FRANCE
POLAND
CZECHO-SLOVAKIA
TURKEY
GREECE
NICARAGUA

Intelligence photos showing Qadaffi, Khameini, Stalin, Hitler, Ivan The Terrible and Genghis Khan meeting at Managua

YES! I want to take advantage of your special 5th year offer to send another $100 million AT NO COST TO ME except another $100 million.

I understand that if I am not completely satisfied with your Contra policy, I can send more money or a couple of my kids.

NAME----------------
ADDRESS-------------

3/19/86

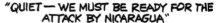

"AS YOU CAN SEE FROM THIS DIAGRAM, DRAWN FROM AN ACTUAL ADVERTISEMENT—"

"QUIET — WE MUST BE READY FOR THE ATTACK BY NICARAGUA"

3/18/86

7/1/86

"I'M GLAD COMMANDANTE CASEY IS BACK IN CHARGE— HE IS VERY SMART ABOUT PERSONAL FINANCES"

"IN WASHINGTON YOU'LL MEET WITH COMMANDANTE GEORGE BUSH. HE'LL BE WEARING A FALSE BEARD AND DESIGNER FATIGUES AND CARRYING A PENNANT THAT SAYS, 'GO CONTRAS!' "

7/25/86

10/15/86

"AND WHAT MAKES YOU THINK WE'D KNOW ANYTHING ABOUT A PLANE GOING DOWN?"

ADMINISTRATION CREDIBILITY

THE DISINFORMATION MEMO

©1986 HERBLOCK

10/8/86

©1986 HERBLOCK

11/11/86

SPARE PARTS

©1986 HERBLOCK

11/14/86

"PIECE OF CAKE"

©1986 HERBLOCK

11/13/86

SCHOOL FOR TERRORISTS

Lesson #1

Grab a hostage and make a powerful western nation jump through hoops.

©1986 HERBLOCK

11/12/86

"YOU HAVE HEARD WILD TALK THAT THERE IS A CAN OF WORMS — THIS IS NOT A CAN OF WORMS — IF IT WAS A CAN OF WORMS, WE WOULD NOT BE IN IT —"

©1986 HERBLOCK

11/16/86

1980
IRAN AND
HOSTAGES

1986
IRAN AND
HOSTAGES

©1986 HERBLOCK

11/19/86

"REPENT, BROTHERS"

REV. REAGAN ADMINISTRATION ON REFORM

SECRET ARMS DEAL

©1986 *Herblock*
11/18/86

"THEY WORK LIKE THE MOTEL NO-VACANCY SIGNS"

NO ARMS TO IRAN

DEALS FOR HOSTAGES

NO

©1986 *Herblock*
11/21/86

"REMEMBER WHEN HE SAID, 'YOU AIN'T SEEN NOTHIN' YET'?"

THE NICARAGUAN CONNECTION

THE IRANIAN ARMS DEALS

©1986 *Herblock*
11/26/86

"MISTAKE? WHAT MISTAKE?"

S.S. CREDIBILITY

©1986 *Herblock*
11/25/86

"MAYBE IT'S BETTER WHEN KHOMEINI MAKES US OUT TO BE THE GREAT SATAN"

©1986 HERBLOCK

11/23/86

"LET THE CHIPS FALL WHERE THEY MAY"

© 1986 HERBLOCK
12/4/86

"WE'RE SECRETLY NEUTRAL"

SECRET ARMS TO IRAN

SECRETS TO IRAQ

©1986 HERBLOCK

12/16/86

ILLEGALITIES

THE CONTRA CONNECTION

SECRET GOVERNMENT

ARMS TO IRAN

MISREPRESENTATIONS

INCOMPETENCE

©1986 HERBLOCK

11/28/86

"I DON'T SUPPOSE ANY HIGH OFFICIALS KNEW ANYTHING, BUT I THOUGHT I'D ASK YOU ANYHOW"

The Iran-Contra Scandal

ADMINISTRATION STALWART EDWIN MEESE

INVESTIGATOR EDWIN MEESE

©1986 HERBLOCK

11/30/86

©1986 HERBLOCK
12/10/86

"LET'S NOT PREJUDGE ANYONE — AND CONGRESS SHOULD GIVE THIS MAN IMMUNITY"

WHEEL OF MISFORTUNE

12/18/86

"WHERE ARE WE NOW?"

12/11/86

"WE WANT TO GET TO THE BOTTOM OF THIS"

©1986 HERBLOCK

12/19/86

179

"SPEAK SOFTLY AND CARRY A BIG STICK"

"THE ONLY THING WE HAVE TO FEAR IS FEAR ITSELF"

"THE BUCK STOPS HERE"

"MISTAKES WERE MADE" by somebody or other —not me— and just in execution of policy or something

©1986 HERBLOCK

12/21/86

"AS FOR REPORTS OF PAPERS DESTROYED, YOU CAN SEE THERE'S NOT A SHRED OF EVIDENCE"

WHITE HOUSE SHREDDING MACHINE

CONFETTI FACTORY

IN CASE OF EMERGENCY, CALL THE FBI, BUT NOT RIGHT AWAY

©1987 HERBLOCK
1/7/87

COVER STORY

ARMS-FOR-HOSTAGES DEALS

If this comes out we'll say we were trying to improve our geostrategic position in the Persian Gulf by seeing moderates in Iran

©1987 HERBLOCK
1/11//87

MISSING
Information wanted on whereabouts of

$ $ MILLIONS $ $
LIKE THE FOUNDING FATHERS

CONTRA FUNDS
=
LAST SEEN WEARING A SWISS HAT AND YODELING

©1987 HERBLOCK
1/14/87

"LET'S GET EVERYTHING OUT IN THE OPEN— WHY DON'T YOU CONGRESSMEN HURRY IT UP?"

©1987 HERBLOCK
1/22/87

LATEST PAYMENT ON THE ARMS SALES

MORE HOSTAGES TAKEN
Iran Presses Offensive in Iraq

©1987 HERBLOCK
1/27/87

Dear Diary:
Today I lashed out again at terrorists. I'm sure glad I don't know anything about the arms we're sending to Iran.

©1987 HERBLOCK
2/3/87

"WHAT'S THE MATTER WITH YOU GUYS—
NO RESPECT FOR US EAGLES?"

JOIN US IN FIGHTING TERRORISM

U.S. ARMS TO IRAN

©1987 HERBLOCK
2/8/87

STATE OF THE UNION

©1987 HERBLOCK
1/23/87

MESSAGE TO TERRORISTS

If you don't return the hostages we will make you another offer

©1987 HERBLOCK

1/30/87

"LET ME JOG YOUR MEMORY A LITTLE"

D Regan account of Iran Deals

R Reagan statements

©1987 HERBLOCK

2/20/87

"A COMMANDER-IN-CHIEF TELLING A LT. COLONEL TO SPEAK UP? GOSH, I THOUGHT THAT MIGHT BE ILLEGAL OR SOMETHING"

Yours, Ollie

Best, John P.

BOLAND AMENDMENT BARRING CONTRA AID

ANTI-TERRORISM ARMS EMBARGO LAW

CONGRESSIONAL OVERSIGHT LAW

©1987 HERBLOCK

2/12/87

"I CAN DELIVER THE LINES AS GOOD AS EVER, BUT THEY KEEP CHANGING THE SCRIPTS ON ME"

©1987 HERBLOCK

2/25/87

"I THOUGHT YOU CAME OFF PRETTY WELL"

CHIEF OF CHAOS

OUT TO LUNCH

TOWER COMMISSION REPORT

Donald Regan

©1987 HERBLOCK
2/27/87

TOWER COMMISSION REPORT

WE DID NOT TRADE WEAPONS OR ANYTHING ELSE FOR HOSTAGES
—Reagan, Nov. 13, 1986

©1987 HERBLOCK
3/1/87

"NO, NO, YOU FIRST — YOU'RE SORT OF A PRIVATE GOVERNMENT"

Banque Suisse

WALL STREET INSIDER STOCK TRADERS

WHITE HOUSE INSIDER ARMS TRADERS

©1987 HERBLOCK
2/8/87

"LOOK AT THE BRIGHT SIDE — WITH SO MANY THINGS WRONG, WHO CAN KEEP TRACK OF THEM?"

WHITE HOUSE STRATEGY DEPT.

MISSTATEMENTS
DECEPTIONS
Latest Disclosures
IRANIAN ARMS DEALS
CONTRA CONNECTION
MISSING FUNDS
SECRET GOVERNMENT
PRIVATE FOREIGN POLICY OPERATIONS
MEMORY LAPSES
OFFICIAL LIES
DON'T-TELL-ANYBODY MEMOS
SWISS BANK ACCOUNTS
Senate Intelligence Committee Report
conflicting testimony
PAPER SHREDDING
TOWER COMMISSION REPORT

©1987 HERBLOCK
3/3/87

©1987 HERBLOCK
3/20/87

© 1987 HERBLOCK

3/5/87

"WE'VE SPENT ENOUGH TIME THE LAST FEW MONTHS ON INSIDE-WASHINGTON POLITICS" —Reagan

IRAN

IRAQ

ISRAEL

SWITZERLAND

DENMARK

PORTUGAL

NICARAGUA

COSTA RICA

BEIRUT

BRUNEI

SAUDI ARABIA

ANYWHERE, U.S.A.

©1987 HERBLOCK

3/6/87

"YOU DON'T REMEMBER EITHER—YOU DON'T REMEMBER EITHER..."

3/27/87

"OBVIOUSLY, A REAL LEGIT OPERATION"

3/18/87

"HOW ABOUT SOME GLASNOST OVER HERE?"

3/29/87

COMMUNICATOR

4/16/87

"THOSE TV NEWS DEPARTMENTS, WASTING ALL THAT TIME AND MONEY — WHY DON'T THEY PUT ON MORE ENTERTAINMENT?"

©1987 HERBLOCK

5/5/87

THE FACE ON THE SHREDDING ROOM FLOOR

©1987 HERBLOCK

4/10/87

WHITE HOUSE TOUR

©1987 HERBLOCK

5/14/87

"HE'S BEEN A COMPLETELY·IN·CHARGE PRESIDENT —HE WAS ABSOLUTELY FIRM ABOUT NOT WANTING THE DETAILS"

IRAN-CONTRA DEALS

5/12/87

"NOTHING—I JUST THOUGHT I HEARD AN ECHO"

WE COULD RAISE THE MONEY, BUT...

IRAN-CONTRA SCANDALS

5/17/87

THE RESTORED PRIDE IN AMERICA

PLEASE GIVE TO OUR WAR AGAINST NICARAGUA

PLEASE HELP TO RANSOM THE HOSTAGES

5/15/87

IRAQI PLANE HITS U.S. WARSHIP

CASUALTIES:

5/19/87

"NOBODY HERE BUT JUST US PATRIOTS"

©1987 HERBLOCK 5/22/87

ALTERED DOCUMENT

5/27/87

6/24/87

6/4/87

WHITE HOUSE BASEMENT

SECRET ARMS-TO-IRAN DEALS

LOSS OF CREDIBILITY

LOSS OF FACE IN ARAB WORLD

KUWAITI-RUSSIAN DEAL

PERSIAN GULF SHIP-FLAGGING MESS

©1987 HERBLOCK
6/17/87

"THERE AIN'T NO SMOKING GUN"–Reagan

North Hall Secord

SHREDDING MACHINE

©1987 HERBLOCK

6/18/87

PANIC BUTTON

6/21/87

"REMEMBER—A LOT OF PEOPLE HAVE DIED FACE DOWN IN THE MUD SO THAT THIS MAN COULD VIOLATE THE LAWS, SHRED EVIDENCE AND TELL CONGRESS HIS CONDITIONS FOR ALLOWING THEM TO SEE HIM"

6/23/87

PEDESTAL

7/9/87

7/8/87

"UP, UP, AND — DOWN! DOWN!"

"I LIKE THAT OLLIE NORTH CROWD—THEY CARE ENOUGH ABOUT DEMOCRACY IN NICARAGUA THAT THEY'RE WILLING TO KICK THE HELL OUT OF IT IN THE U.S."

©1987 HERBLOCK

7/10/87

"NOW, AGAIN, THAT FAMOUS TEAM—"

IRAN—CONTRA HEARINGS

Hatch and Hyde The Apologists

© 1987 HERBLOCK
7/14/87

"NOW WE'VE GOT A LOT OF FACTS — BUT SOME FROM PEOPLE WHO HAVE DONE A LOT OF LYING"

IRAN-CONTRA COMMITTEE

© 1987 HERBLOCK
7/21/87

"I TAKE MY HAT OFF TO YOU FELLOWS"

© 1987 HERBLOCK
7/29/87

CARD FILE

MEESE NOTES

© 1987 HERBLOCK
7/30/87

"SEE, THEY HAD TO USE SO MUCH SECRECY AND DECEPTION BECAUSE WHAT THEY WERE DOING WAS SO LEGAL AND STRAIGHTFORWARD"

7/19/87

"STAY TUNED — FOLLOWING THE HEARINGS THERE WILL BE A TELETHON"

PLEDGE TO THE JOHN POINDEXTER AMNESIA FUND

HELP RESTORE THE MEMORIES OF THESE MEN

7/22/87

THE ULTIMATE COVER-UP

Wᴹ J. CASEY

IRAN-CONTRA

7/12/87

"LET ME GUESS—IT'S A PROCLAMATION FOR NATIONAL APPLE PIE WEEK"

©1987 HERBLOCK

7/16/87

"I'M NOT ABOUT TO LET THE DUST AND COBWEBS SETTLE ON THE FURNITURE IN THIS OFFICE..."

8/14/87

"AHOY, THERE — ARE YOU MODERATES?"

8/5/87

"IT'S FROM OUR SON — HE'S JUGGLING MINES FOR THE EMIR OF KUWAIT"

8/16/87

"Q. WHAT HAVE WE LEARNED FROM IRAN-CONTRA? A. We didn't carry the secrecy obsession far enough."

8/12/87

Dear Candidate:

I understand you fellows like to get a feel of what the voters are concerned about. I can tell you about some things that concern me besides front-page front-burner items like official corruption.

For the last few years we've been hearing a lot about what a great power we are, and we're Number 1, and it's morning in America, and we're the greatest in the world.

I haven't traveled enough to know how it is in all the other countries, but I know how it used to be *here*.

There are lots of things missing besides nickel candy bars and penny licorice shoestrings. You used to be able to mail a letter for less than 22 cents and expect it to get across town or in a nearby city in a day or so—special delivery, if you wanted it there next morning. They don't even *have* special delivery any more—it would probably just slow up service even more while they waited for a kid with a bike. Now you can get first-class letters many days late. You can still get overnight service—for about eleven bucks. But you have to take it to a post office for that.

Meanwhile the junk mail piles up and burdens the postal employees. A lot of not-very-personal first-class mail comes from businesses that get special low rates from the postal department. They can't tell me all this stuff doesn't slow up the real letters from real people to other real people. It does, and I can see it on the postmarks. I also see it on invitations mailed in plenty of time, which arrive after the events.

You used to be able to get on a plane and expect it to take off on time and at least come close to arriving on time. Have you gone anywhere by plane lately—I mean, aside from special junkets and military planes and Air Force One? You know what I'm talking about. Deregulation shmeregulation. Don't tell me we can't do anything to get travel back on schedule in this country.

We're now down to one major bus line. And trains aren't what they used to be either. If the railroads were improved, maybe more people would ride them, and they'd even take some of the load off the planes. I understand that in Europe and Japan they have trains that go like hell. Canada has some fine ones too. We're not Number 1 in travel, are we?

Autos—they're our biggest form of transportation. Have you tried to get yours serviced lately—and at a decent price? Frankly, most of my friends are buying imports—they say those run better, last longer and need less servicing. We hear a lot about "competitiveness," which seems to be kind of a synonym for protectionism. What about competitiveness in quality? What happened to our big lead in the auto business?

All that is just transportation. What about telephones? Since the breakup of the old phone company, I get so many bills with so many itemizations for so many special charges that pretty soon they're going to have to send these bills bound like books. We spend more money on outgoing calls and more time with unwelcome incoming calls. The junk phone solicitations, like the junk mail, keep coming through.

The TV ads tell us that the pride is back. Okay, I'm all for pride. It's fine that there's pride in the military service, for example. But how about everyday non-military just-plain *service*—the old customer-is-right idea. Private service and government service have not been Number 1 lately.

And speaking of government—something else that bothers me: What about NASA—what happened to our once-spectacular space program? What happened to safety precautions and backup systems and all? Private companies in the U.S. have negotiated with China about launching satellites into space for them. China! And the Russians have taken ads in our newspapers to tell us that *their* launch service is the most reliable for us to use. Talk about competitiveness! Well, I'll bet we're still Number 1 in ad agencies, anyhow.

Now, what about the environment? What's happening with acid rain, with the ozone layer, with nuclear waste? My neighborhood hasn't yet turned into a dump, but I think the government ought to be doing something more than spinning a wheel to see what areas get dumped on. The environment I'm familiar with is closer to home. I don't like smog and pollution; and I hope they put in more no-smoking areas in restaurants and other public places. With clean air, I breathe better.

I'd also breathe easier if I didn't keep reading about crime, more of that closer to home, too. Most of it seems to involve handguns. In addition to smog and tobacco smoke we have lots of gunsmoke. In all the world we're absolutely and unquestionably Number 1 in guns and gun fatalities. Maybe you fellows in government can do something about this. I don't like the feeling that we're like some shoot-em-up frontier town or a ho-hum banana republic.

We also seem to be Number 1 in stock trading and greenmail and things like that. I don't know much about Wall Street or how those big deals are managed. But I know about places I see. In the area where I travel several Safeway stores have closed. That happened after a take-over threat where the fellows who threatened the takeover walked off with over $100 million. And all apparently legit. So we have fewer stores and a lot of people who worked in them are now unemployed.

Big gamblers used to talk about keeping the grocery clerks out. I guess that's what some of the financial gamblers are doing. Clerks' jobs and stores—out. And consumers too. Somebody has to pay for that $100 million. Right?

If somebody can pick up that kind of money from being clever with computers, we ought to have people in government who are smart enough and care enough to figure how to stop that kind of game.

At one time some snobbish people in Europe used to call us a nation of dollar-chasers; they talked about "the almighty dollar." It wasn't true then. But now maybe it is. Remember what Vince Lombardi said about winning? It's not everything—it's the *only* thing. It's getting to be like that with money. It's especially that way among the big shots. They've often talked about how poor people have needed to develop a "work ethic." A lot of high rollers have developed what I'd call a Greed Ethic. I guess that combination of words is what some columnists would call an oxymoron, but it fits.

Well, if you're elected, I'd like you to do something about the Greed Ethic. I know you can't do everything, but you can make a beginning. You can set a tone. You can talk about a Service Ethic.

You can keep in mind Harry Truman's words: The buck stops here. And you can add something else: Anything-for-a-buck stops *now*.

"WE WERE JUST GOING OVER OUR LATEST STUDY, WHEN SOMEONE STEPPED OUTSIDE WITH IT"

©1984 HERBLOCK

9/2/84

"IF IT DOESN'T CARRY MISSILES, WHAT GOOD IS IT?"

©1985 HERBLOCK

2/27/85

"HELLO—DO I GET TO VOTE ON RETURNING TO THE OLD TELEPHONE SYSTEM?—HELLO—HELLO?"

©1985 HERBLOCK

10/13/85

"I SAY LET'S GET TO THE ROOT OF THE PROBLEM AND MAKE THEM STOP TURNING OUT BETTER PRODUCTS"

4/22/87

COMMEMORATIVE STAMP

12/13/84

BLIND

12/28/86

12/1/85

©1986 HERBLOCK

4/27/86

NASA
CONTRACT
OVERSPENDING
DEPT.

NASA
POLITICS AND
P.R. DEPT.

QUALITY CONTROL
AND SAFETY
DEPT.

5/11/86

"IT SAYS HERE THE U.S. IS GOING TO TAKE PART IN ANOTHER STUDY OF ACID RAIN"

3/20/85

THE PUSHERS

DRUG DEALER

NRA HANDGUN LOBBY

8/21/86

ENVIRONMENTAL PROGRAM

KEEP SMILING

TOXIC DUMPS

11/4/84

©1986 HERBLOCK

11/20/86

"TRADE RESTRICTIONS MAKE IMPORTS COST MORE; THEN WE <u>COMPETE</u> — WE BOOST OUR PRICES TO MATCH"

5/24/87

"DAMNED LAW OBSERVER!"

12/2/84

"I DON'T KNOW WHY THEY DON'T SEEM TO HOLD US IN AWE THE WAY THEY USED TO"

6/16/87

"YOU MIGHT NEED A NEW KIND OF ADVERTISING"

8/31/84

"HELP — GASP — I CAN'T STAND THAT CLEAN AIR OVER THERE"

7/6/86

"THOSE MEXICAN FOREIGNERS DOWN THERE ARE RAISING STUFF THAT'S DANGEROUS"

6/25/86

12/15/85

10/9/86

"AMTRAK? MASS TRANSIT? WHO NEEDS THEM?"

OFFICIAL PLANE

OFFICIAL LIMO

©1985 HERBLOCK

4/23/85

HOLIDAY SEASON LIST

The gift that keeps on radiating

NUCLEAR WASTE SITES

ENERGY DEPT.

©1984 HERBLOCK

12/23/84

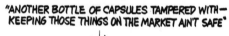

"ANOTHER BOTTLE OF CAPSULES TAMPERED WITH—
KEEPING THOSE THINGS ON THE MARKET AIN'T SAFE"

SALE ON HANDGUNS

GUNS AND AMMO

NRA SPECIAL

©1986 HERBLOCK

3/25/86

"WELL, THAT SOLVES THE ACID RAIN PROBLEM FOR A WHILE"

1/18/85

"AND THE WINNERS OF TODAY'S LOTTERY FOR 8 O'CLOCK TAKEOFF—"

9/9/84

"WHY SHOULDN'T THEY PAY AMATEUR ATHLETES? HOW ELSE CAN THEY AFFORD THOSE DRUGS?"

4/5/87